CONTENTS

P9-CQS-609

DESIGNED BY GAMES WORKSHOP IN NOTTINGHAM

With thanks to the Faithful and the Warhammer Age of Sigmar community for their playtesting services.

Games Workshop Ltd., Willow Road, Lenton, Nottingham, NG7 2WS, United Kingdom
games-workshop.com

TO WAR!

Welcome to the *General's Handbook 2018* – a guide to playing games in the Mortal Realms. Packed with inspiration and brimming with battles, this volume is the key to a treasure chest of different ways to enjoy Warhammer Age of Sigmar.

This book expands on the Warhammer Age of Sigmar core rules to support an array of gaming styles that suit all hobbyists, from casual collectors who play occasional games with their friends to veteran warriors who spend years honing their forces for competitive tournaments.

Everyone enjoys the Games Workshop hobby in different ways. Some hobbyists are avid painters who collect stunning centrepiece models, and others spend their hobby time reading the background and learning the lore. For some, though, using their collections to play games against like-minded opponents across the tabletop is at the very heart of their hobby. If you fall into the latter category, then this book is for you, as it focuses on that aspect of the hobby where the miniatures meet the battlefield.

It is important to note that all of the rules presented in this book are optional; they can be used, or not, in any combination that you and your tabletop adversaries find enjoyable. To this end, the *General's Handbook 2018* has been designed to work as a gaming toolbox, providing many options to get the dice rolling and play with your collection of Citadel Miniatures on the tabletop. For instance, there are updated warscrolls for Citadel terrain features, options for waging warfare in the skies, rules for historical and large-scale battles, as well as many new battleplans and Open War tables for generating your own.

The different ways to combine the rules in this book are practically endless, and this flexible system ensures that, whether you are just getting started or have decades of experience, everyone can find a style of play that suits them. So, if you and your gaming group want to stage an enormous battle with balanced forces using a bespoke battleplan made from the Open War tables, you can do just that. If you want to play out a story in which armies of flying monsters and sky-vessels engage in grim battle above fields packed with masses of enchanted scenery, then so long as you all agree on the game you're playing beforehand, that's the way to go. Whether you've just picked up your first Start Collecting! box or are dusting off a collection from days long past, the *General's Handbook 2018* is here to help you find your favourite way of playing and give you the tools to bring the Mortal Realms to life on the tabletop.

The first three sections of this book provide rules for three different gaming styles: open play, narrative play, and matched play. Open play is the first type of play that is covered, and it is the most flexible style because it can be as simple or as complex as you like. Simply pick any Citadel Miniatures and start playing. The open play section (pg 4-13) includes a guide for creating your own Open War battleplans, with tables upon which you can roll to generate objectives for your games, as well as various twists and turns that will occur amidst the battle. Following this are rules for fighting vertiginous combats in the skies, with two pre-made battleplans suited to aerial warfare.

Narrative play is based around the stories of the Mortal Realms, either those you can read in our books or those you write yourself. Narrative play can involve one-off games fought between mighty heroes, or multiple games linked in a campaign. In the narrative play section (pg 14-43) you will find a suite of special rules that you can pick and choose from when planning your narrative games. Two example historical battles are then presented, each of which has a battleplan that utilises some of these special rules to recreate the conditions and circumstances that affected their outcomes. Following the historical battles is the Gathering of Might sub-section, which provides rules for staging epic-scale battles involving hundreds of combatants.

Matched play allows for armies to be tested against each other under conditions that give no particular advantage to either side, to see which army is strongest and which general is canniest. These styles are fluid, and their component parts can often be used together depending on what you are trying to achieve. The matched play section (pg 44-87) contains a wide array of battleplans, each of which offers a level playing field upon which you can wage war. Following these is a comprehensive list of up-to-date points for every unit, with which you can form your army for tournaments and competitive play.

The final section of this book is called Conquest Unbound (pg 88-137), and offers rules that inject even more excitement and flavour into your games. Included are warscrolls for Citadel scenery models that allow you to use terrain features to augment your battlefields, as well as updated allegiance abilities for various factions.

Whatever style of play you choose, there is no right or wrong way to play Warhammer Age of Sigmar, so long as everyone adheres to the Most Important Rule. We're all here to have fun, after all!

THE MOST IMPORTANT RULE

In a game as detailed and wide-ranging as Warhammer Age of Sigmar, there may be times when you are not sure exactly how to resolve a situation that has come up during play.

When this happens, have a quick chat with your opponent, and apply the solution that makes the most sense to you both (or seems the most fun!).

If no single solution presents itself, both of you should roll a dice, and whoever rolls higher gets to choose what happens. This means you can swiftly and easily resolve the issue, allowing you both to get on with the fighting!

3

OPEN PLAY GAMES

The best ideas are usually the simplest, and open play games of Warhammer Age of Sigmar epitomise this philosophy. Open play is a style of gaming that allows you to take to the battlefield with any army, made up of any Citadel Miniatures from your collection – with no restrictions. It's as straightforward, streamlined and elegant as wargaming gets.

All you need to play an open play game are your painted miniatures, their warscrolls, the Warhammer Age of Sigmar core rules, a battleplan, a set of dice, a tape measure, and a flat surface on which to play. Then, just set up your models and begin the battle! You can add extra dimensions to your open play games by incorporating any of the rules or guidelines that appear in this and other Warhammer Age of Sigmar books, such as allegiance abilities and Realm of Battle rules, or even Pitched Battle points values if you wish. Alternatively, you can conjure up your own scenarios, create new special rules or adapt existing ones to suit your needs.

The flexible nature of open play means that you can spend as long or as little time as you like reading rules, and in its simplest form, it's a great introduction to the world of tabletop games. It is also ideal for those thinking of starting new collections, as it allows battles to be fought with just a few units of the models you plan to collect, so that you can see how they perform on the tabletop.

Open play games allow the broadest choice of army selection, allowing the greatest degree of freedom for collecting miniatures and building an army. You can be inspired by the diverse and mystical nature of the realms, or simply collect the models you most want. If you're the proud owner of a varied collection of warriors, beasts and war machines, there's nothing to stop you fielding all of them in a single game. You can even deploy every last miniature you own, or set yourself unusual challenges. For instance, you could discover how many Stormcast Eternal Liberators it takes to bring down your friend's Khorne Bloodthirster, or maybe see how long a Lord-Celestant can fight off the noxious attentions of a Nurgling horde.

With so much scope for fun and creativity, open play is one of the most accessible and enjoyable gaming styles. On the following pages we provide you with a number of ways to set up and play different types of open play games. All you need to do is grab your miniatures and get playing!

OPEN WAR BATTLEPLAN GENERATOR

The Open War battleplan generator tables are designed for players that like the ease and simplicity of open play games, and are looking for as much variety as possible. If you use them, no two games will ever be exactly the same.

You can use these new tables instead of, or in addition to, those found in the *Warhammer Age of Sigmar Core Book* or the Warhammer Age of Sigmar: Open War cards deck.

Instead of picking a battleplan from a Warhammer Age of Sigmar publication, you can generate your own. This battleplan generator is made up of five tables, which are used to determine how the armies are set up (the Map table), what the players must do in order to win the battle (the Objective and Sudden Death tables), and if any special rules apply to the battle (the Ruse and Twist tables).

THE GENERATOR TABLES

Pick armies and set up terrain as described in the core rules. Then roll on the Map, Objectives, Twist, Ruse and Sudden Death generator tables as described below.

MAP

One player rolls a dice to determine which Map table is used: on an even roll, the map will be generated from Map table 1 (right); on an odd roll, the map will be generated from Map table 2 (far right). Their opponent then rolls a dice and looks up the result on the appropriate Map table. This is the map for this battle.

OBJECTIVES

One player rolls a dice and looks up the result on the Objective table (pg 8). This is the objective for this battle. Sometimes the Objective table will require the player to set up one or more objectives on the battlefield. If both players are required to set up objectives, roll off, and then alternate setting the objectives up starting with the player that won the roll-off.

TWIST

One player rolls a dice and looks up the result on the Twist table (pg 8). The resulting special rule applies for the duration of the battle.

RUSES & SUDDEN DEATH VICTORY CONDITIONS

Each player must add up the Wounds characteristics of all of the models in their army. If one army has a total that is greater than the other, then the player with the lower total is allowed to roll on the Ruse table (pg 9). That ruse can only be used by the player that rolled it. If one army has a total that is at least double the other, then the player with the lower total is allowed to roll on the Sudden Death table (pg 9) as well. That victory condition applies only to the player that rolled it.

> **Designer's Note:** *If they wish, when a player generates a Ruse or Sudden Death victory condition, they can choose to keep the result secret until it comes into play. There are many ways to do this, such as rolling the dice and keeping it hidden beneath a cup.*

SET-UP

The players roll off and the winner decides which territory each side will use. After doing so, the players alternate setting up units wholly within their own territory, one at a time, starting with the player that won the roll-off to pick territories.

GLORIOUS VICTORY

In order to win a **major victory** a player must either achieve the victory conditions rolled on the Objective table, or the one they rolled on the Sudden Death table. Any other result is a draw.

MAP TABLE 1

D6

1

PLAYER A
TERRITORY

12"

PLAYER B
TERRITORY

2

PLAYER A
TERRITORY

12"

PLAYER B
TERRITORY

3

PLAYER A
TERRITORY

PLAYER B
TERRITORY

4

PLAYER A
TERRITORY

12"

12"

PLAYER B
TERRITORY

5

PLAYER A
TERRITORY

PLAYER B
TERRITORY

6

PLAYER A
TERRITORY

PLAYER B
TERRITORY

18"   18"

MAP TABLE 2

D6

1

PLAYER A TERRITORY

12"

18"

PLAYER B
TERRITORY

2

PLAYER A
TERRITORY

PLAYER A
TERRITORY

PLAYER B
TERRITORY

3

PLAYER B TERRITORY

PLAYER A
TERRITORY

PLAYER B TERRITORY

12"   24"   12"

4

PLAYER A
TERRITORY

PLAYER A
TERRITORY

PLAYER B
TERRITORY

24"

PLAYER A
TERRITORY

PLAYER A
TERRITORY

5

PLAYER A TERRITORY

12"

12"

PLAYER B TERRITORY

6

PLAYER A
TERRITORY

12"   12"

PLAYER B
TERRITORY

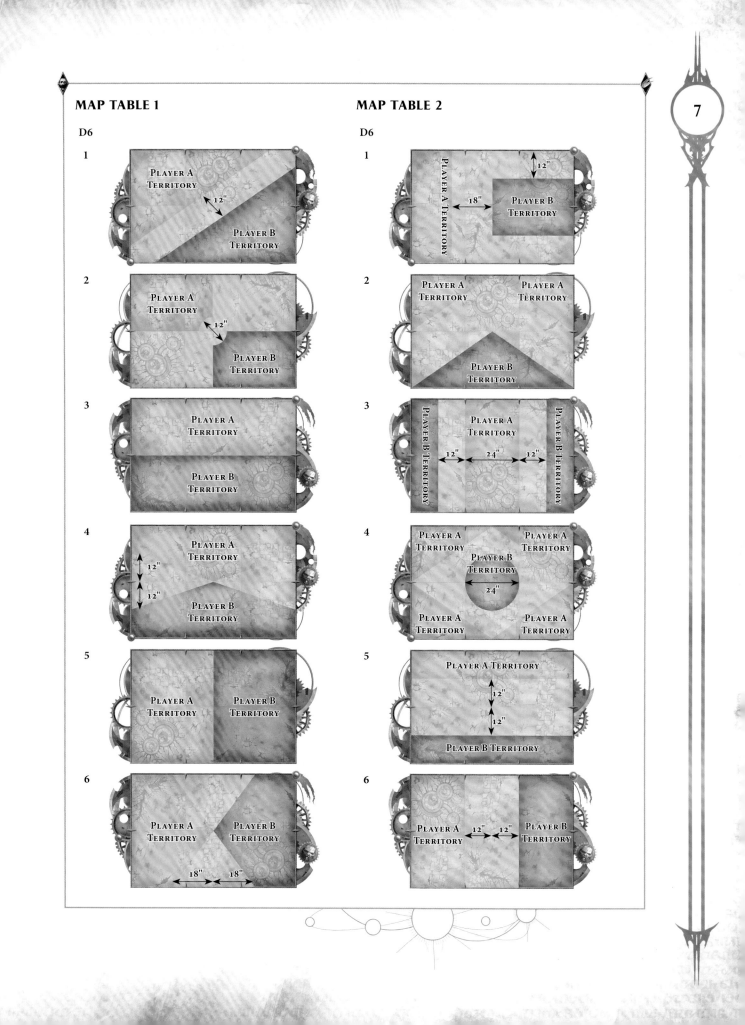

OBJECTIVE TABLE

D6 Objective

1 Witch Hunt: Each player adds up the Wounds characteristics of all enemy models that their army slays during the battle, doubling the value for any models that have the **WIZARD** keyword. At the end of the fifth battle round, the player with the highest total wins a **major victory** (even if their own army has been wiped out).

2 Contest of Champions: Each player adds up the Wounds characteristics of all enemy models that their army slays during the battle, doubling the value for any models slain by a **HERO** from their army. At the end of the fifth battle round, the player with the highest total wins a **major victory** (even if their own army has been wiped out).

3 Secure a Foothold: All terrain features count as objectives. Players score 1 victory point for each terrain feature they control at the end of the fifth battle round. Buildings that can be garrisoned are worth 2 victory points instead if one of the controlling units is garrisoning the building. The player with the most victory points wins a **major victory**.

4 Domination: The players roll off. Starting with the winner, they take it in turns to set up three objectives each, anywhere wholly within their own territory that is more than 6" from any other objective and the edge of the battlefield. At the end of the fifth battle round, the player that controls the most objectives wins a **major victory**.

5 Flying the Colours: Players score 1 victory point for each enemy unit that their army slays during the battle. Slain enemy units that have the **TOTEM** keyword are worth 2 victory points instead. At the end of the fifth battle round, the player with the highest total wins a **major victory** (even if their own army has been wiped out).

6 Meteor Shower: Roll three dice at the start of the third battle round after determining who has the first turn, re-rolling any duplicates until all three scores are different. Place an objective as close as possible to the centre of the three corresponding locations shown on the map on the right. At the end of the fifth battle round, the player that controls the most objectives wins a **major victory**.

TWIST TABLE

D6 Twist

1 Unstable Ground: Subtract 1 from the Move characteristic of all models, and subtract 1 from all run and charge rolls (to a minimum of 1). In addition, if a double 6 is rolled for a charge roll, the charging unit suffers D3 mortal wounds.

2 Foreboding Environment: Subtract 1 from the Bravery characteristic of all models.

3 Judgement of the Gods: Each time a unit fails a battleshock test, it suffers D3 mortal wounds at the end of that phase, but does not have to take a battleshock test in the following turn.

4 Howling Winds: Subtract 1 from hit rolls made for missile weapons that target enemy models at over half of their maximum range. In addition, each time a unit uses its ability to fly (to move over terrain, for example), subtract D6 from its Move characteristic (to a minimum of 1) for the duration of that phase.

5 Hail of Teeth: Each time a unit fails a battleshock test, one additional model from that unit flees.

6 Quicksand: At the start of each of your opponent's hero phases, pick up to three of their units. For the rest of their turn, each time your opponent rolls a 1 when running with one of the units you picked, or rolls a 1 on either dice when making a charge roll for one of the units you picked, one model from that unit is slain.

Meteor Shower Objectives Map

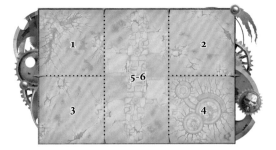

RUSE TABLE

D6   Ruse

1   **Inspired Leadership:** As long as your general is on the battlefield, you receive 1 extra command point at the start of each of your hero phases.

2   **Catch Them Off Guard:** Use this ruse after set-up is complete, but before the battle begins. You can immediately move any of your units up to D6" (roll separately for each unit).

3   **Adaptive Strategy:** You can use this ruse once per battle, at the end of any turn. You receive 1 command point for each of your units that was destroyed that turn.

4   **Counter-charge:** You can use this ruse once per battle, at the end of your opponent's charge phase. Pick a unit in your army that is more than 3" from any enemy models. You can attempt to make a charge move with that unit as if it were your charge phase.

5   **Marked for Death:** You can use this ruse once per battle, after picking a unit from your army to attack with missile weapons. Pick an eligible enemy **HERO** within range to target; the Look Out, Sir! rule does not apply when resolving these attacks.

6   **Oath of War:** Use this ruse after set-up is complete, but before the battle begins. Pick a unit from your army. The unit cannot be a **HERO** or **MONSTER** and must already be set up on the battlefield. Ignore negative modifiers when making their save rolls for the duration of the battle. However, this effect ends immediately if any models from the unit flee as a result of a failed battleshock test.

SUDDEN DEATH TABLE

D6   Sudden Death Victory Condition

1   **A Glorious Death:** You immediately win a **major victory** if your army is wiped out before the end of the third battle round.

2   **Slay Their Leaders:** You immediately win a **major victory** if a unit from your army slays the last enemy **HERO** on the battlefield.

3   **Protect the Messenger:** At the start of the first battle round, before determining who has the first turn, pick one model in your army to be the messenger. The model cannot be your army's general and must already be set up on the battlefield. You immediately win a **major victory** if your messenger is still on the battlefield at the end of the fourth battle round.

4   **Crippling Blow:** You immediately win a **major victory** if you destroy the enemy unit that has the highest combined Wounds characteristic of any enemy unit that is currently on the battlefield (if several have the same combined Wounds characteristic, you win if any of them is destroyed).

5   **Destined for Greatness:** You immediately win a **major victory** if your general is still on the battlefield at the end of the third battle round.

6   **Take the Fight to Them:** Starting from the third battle round, you immediately win a **major victory** if three or more of your units are wholly within your opponent's territory.

AERIAL BATTLES

If you have lots of units that can fly in your collection and like the idea of adding a different dimension to your games of Warhammer Age of Sigmar, you can fight an Aerial Battle. In such games, airborne creatures and creations of all shapes and sizes clash against one another in vertiginous battles far above the ground.

There are two types of Aerial Battle: Overhead Aerial Battles and Stratospheric Aerial Battles. The following rule applies to both types of Aerial Battle.

Fleet of Wing: *Aerial combat is swift and deadly, with adversaries on both sides darting along on jet streams and magical currents to launch free-wheeling attacks against their foes.*

Units on an aerial battlefield that can fly can be picked to fight when they are within 6" of an enemy unit and can pile in up to 6". In addition, units on an aerial battlefield that can fly can charge even if they retreated earlier in the turn.

OVERHEAD AERIAL BATTLES

In this version, two battlefields are used; one representing the ground level, where ground-based units fight (the ground battlefield), and the other representing the skies above the battlefield in which an aerial skirmish is taking place (the aerial battlefield). This type of game is great if you don't want to leave out all your ground-based units but still want to explore the exciting dynamics of airborne conflict.

With the exception of the following rules, which apply to all Overhead Aerial Battles, units on one battlefield cannot interact in any way (i.e. command abilities, spells, etc.) with units on the other battlefield.

Ground Volleys: *Troops on the ground can take speculative pot-shots at enemies flying overhead, though they rely more on luck than skill to hit their mark.*

Units on the ground battlefield can target enemy units on the aerial battlefield with missile weapons that have a Range characteristic of 18" or more. However, a 6 is always required for a successful hit roll, irrespective of the firing model's To Hit characteristic or any modifiers.

Raining Bodies: *As war rages overhead, the bodies of the slain fall like macabre rain, crushing the unwary fighting below.*

Each time a unit on the aerial battlefield is destroyed, players take it in turns to pick an enemy unit on the ground battlefield and roll a dice (starting with the player that destroyed the unit on the aerial battlefield). On a 6, the unit being rolled for suffers 1 mortal wound, or D3 mortal wounds if the destroyed unit was a **Monster**. Players continue rolling in this manner until each unit on the ground battlefield has been rolled for once, or until a unit on the ground battlefield suffers any mortal wounds, whichever occurs sooner.

Upon the Wings of Death: *Winged warriors and flying beasts are able to soar high and swoop low, lending their strength and speed wherever it is needed most.*

Only units that can fly can be set up on the aerial battlefield. In your movement phase, units that can fly can switch battlefields instead of moving. Remove the unit from play and set it up anywhere on the other battlefield so that is it more than 9" away from any enemy units.

STRATOSPHERIC AERIAL BATTLES

In this format, only the aerial battle is represented, using just one battlefield (the aerial battlefield), and non-flying units are positioned atop towering spires or other lofty structures so that they can aid their flying brethren.

The following rules apply to all Stratospheric Aerial Battles:

Long Way Up: *Those bold enough to brave the heights can climb atop rocky outcrops and towering spires to lend what aid they can to their winged brethren.*

Units that are unable to fly can only be set up as garrisons of buildings or other terrain features wholly within their territory. These units cannot leave the buildings they are garrisoning; if forced to do so for any reason, they count as slain.

Long Way Down: *For those that lack the freedom of flight, there is a chance that even a harmless gust will see them lose balance and fall from their precarious positions, causing them to tumble to their death far below.*

At the start of the battleshock phase, roll a dice for each non-flying enemy unit that passed any save rolls earlier in the turn. On a 1 one model in that unit is slain. Models slain in this manner count towards the unit's battleshock test.

AERIAL BATTLE BATTLEPLANS

On the following pages, you will find two example battleplans that demonstrate these two methods of play.

You can also use Open War tables to generate your own battleplan. If you want to play a Overhead Aerial Battle, generate a map for each battlefield using the Map table on page 7, or generate a single map and use the same map for both battlefields. If you want to play a Stratospheric Aerial Battle, simply generate one map as normal. Then, generate an Objective and Twist from the Aerial Battle tables opposite. Finally, generate a Ruse and, if applicable, a Sudden Death victory condition as normal from the Ruse and Sudden Death tables on page 9.

AERIAL BATTLES OBJECTIVE TABLE

D6 **Objective**

1 **Clear the Skies:** Players score 1 victory point for each enemy unit that their army slays during the battle. Slain enemy units that can fly are worth 2 victory points instead. At the end of the fifth battle round, the player with the highest total wins a **major victory** (even if their own army has been wiped out).

2 **Control the Heights:** All terrain features count as objectives. Players score 1 victory point for each objective they control at the end of the fifth battle round. Buildings that can be garrisoned are worth 2 victory points instead if they are garrisoned by a unit that cannot fly. The player with the most victory points wins a **major victory**.

3 **Winged Messenger:** At the start of the first battle round, before determining who has the first turn, each player lets their opponent know which model in their army is their messenger. The model cannot be the army's general, must already be set up on the battlefield and must be able to fly. The first player to slay their opponent's messenger wins a **major victory**.

4 **Hunt for the Skyshard:** All terrain features count as objectives. At the start of each player's turn, they must roll a dice for each objective they control, in any order they wish. If they roll a 6, they have found the skyshard – all other terrain features no longer count as objectives. The player that controls the skyshard objective at the end of the fifth battle round wins a **major victory**.

5 **Fire in the Sky:** At the start of the first battle round, before determining who has the first turn, each player picks between one and three terrain features anywhere on the battlefield (though both players must pick the same number). These terrain features count as objectives. A player can set light to any enemy objectives that they control at the end of their turn. The first player to set light to all of the enemy's objectives wins a **major victory**.

6 **Aerial Dominance:** Each player adds up the Wounds characteristics of all enemy models that their army slays during the battle, doubling the value for any models that have the **MONSTER** keyword and can fly. At the end of the fifth battle round, the player with the highest total wins a **major victory** (even if their own army has been wiped out).

AERIAL BATTLES TWIST TABLE

D6 **Twist**

1 **Harassing Tactics:** Before set-up, each player rolls a D6 for each of their units. On a 6, that unit is placed to one side. At the end of any of their movement phases after the first, the controlling player can set up these units anywhere wholly within their territory, wholly within 9" of the battlefield edge and more than 9" from any enemy models.

2 **Wild Lightning:** In each of their hero phases, the player whose turn is taking place can pick up to three enemy units that can fly and roll a dice for each of them. On a 6, the unit being rolled for suffers D3 mortal wounds.

3 **Stormy Skies:** Subtract 1 from hit rolls made for missile weapons that target enemy models at over half of their maximum range. In addition, for the purposes of the Long Way Down rule (see opposite), a model is slain on a roll of 1 or 2, instead of only 1.

4 **Eye of the Hurricane:** At the start of each hero phase, roll a dice for any model within 6" of the edge of the battlefield. On a 1, that model is slain.

5 **Burning Sky:** At the start of each battle round, roll a dice for each unit on the aerial battlefield that is not garrisoning a building, adding 1 to the result if the unit includes 5 or more models. On a 6+ that unit suffers 1 mortal wound. Note that this Twist has no effect on units that are on the ground battlefield in Overhead Aerial Battles.

6 **Smothering Ash Cloud:** The range of all command abilities, spells, missile weapons and other abilities is reduced to 12".

Kharadron Overlords
Endrinrigger

BATTLEPLAN
BY LAND AND AIR

This land is home to an enemy that has long controlled the skies. To ensure your dominance of this region, victory must be won both on the ground and in the skies above it.

OVERHEAD AERIAL BATTLE

Use the Overhead Aerial Battle rules on page 10.

THE BATTLEFIELD

This battleplan requires the players to set up two battlefields: a ground battlefield and an aerial battlefield, an example of which is shown below. However, you may wish to use the Open War battleplan generator to determine the map(s) instead (pg 7). The two battlefields can be of equal size, though this is not strictly necessary. You may even want to use a sheet of blue cloth to represent the aerial battlefield. Set up terrain on the ground battlefield as normal. On the aerial battlefield, you may wish to use a scattering of terrain pieces to serve as especially tall towers, trees or rocky outcrops towering into the sky – though you can just as readily leave it barren to represent open sky.

SET-UP

Generate a Twist from the Aerial Battles Twist table on page 11, as well as a Ruse and – if applicable – a Sudden Death victory condition from the Ruse and Sudden Death tables on page 9.

The players then set up their armies as described in the core rules and the Overhead Aerial Battle rules on page 10.

COMMAND OF THE SKIES

Achieving aerial dominance in this region grants a significant tactical edge, allowing a commander to utilise their control of the skies to execute even more daring strategies and manoeuvres.

If you control the aerial battlefield (see right) at the start of your hero phase, you receive 1 extra command point that phase.

VICTORY

The game lasts for five battle rounds unless a sudden death victory condition is met, in which case the game ends immediately and that player wins a **major victory**.

Otherwise, the battle is fought for control of the two battlefields. A player controls a battlefield if they have more models on it than their opponent. Each **Monster** counts as a number of models equal to its Wounds characteristic for this purpose. If both players have the same number of models on a battlefield, that battlefield is contested.

If one player controls both battlefields at the end of the game, that player wins a **major victory**. If one player controls one battlefield and the other is contested at the end of the game, that player wins a **minor victory**. If both battlefields are contested at the end of the game, the result is a **draw**. If both battlefields are controlled by different players at the end of the game, the result is a **draw**.

GROUND BATTLEFIELD   AERIAL BATTLEFIELD

PLAYER A TERRITORY   PLAYER A TERRITORY

PLAYER B TERRITORY   PLAYER B TERRITORY

BATTLEPLAN
DEATH ON THE WING

The Mortal Realms are replete with many weird and wonderful creatures and inventions that can take to the skies, be it upon feathered pinions or invisible tides of aetheric energy. Battles fought between them for dominance of the skies are always swift and brutal affairs.

STRATOSPHERIC AERIAL BATTLE

Use the Stratospheric Aerial Battle rules on page 10.

THE BATTLEFIELD

The entire battlefield is an aerial battlefield, so you may wish to use a piece of blue fabric to represent the sky. Because any non-flying units can only be set up garrisoning terrain features, you may wish to limit any terrain features you use to ones that can be garrisoned. Alternatively, if you have other suitable terrain features in your collection, you can simply agree with your opponent which terrain features represent sufficiently tall, monolithic structures that can be garrisoned.

An example map is shown below, though you may wish to use the Open War battleplan generator to determine the map instead (pg 7).

SET-UP

Generate a Twist from the Aerial Battles Twist table on page 11, as well as a Ruse and – if applicable – a Sudden Death victory condition from the Ruse and Sudden Death tables on page 9.

The players then set up their armies as described in the core rules and the Stratospheric Aerial Battle rules on page 10.

SKYBORNE LORD

If your general can fly, you can use the following command ability:

Raptor Strike: You can use this command ability after piling in with a friendly unit that charged earlier in the turn and that is wholly within 12" of your general. You can re-roll failed hit rolls for that unit this phase.

VICTORY

If a sudden death victory condition is met, the battle ends immediately and that player wins a **major victory**.

Otherwise, the battle is fought for control of the skies and ends when one player has no units that can fly left on the battlefield, or at the end of the fifth battle round should this occur sooner.

If one player has no models that can fly left on the battlefield, the battle ends and their opponent wins a **major victory**. If both players have models that can fly on the battlefield at the end of the fifth battle round, the player with the most models that can fly on the battlefield wins a **minor victory**. Each MONSTER that can fly counts as a number of models equal to its Wounds characteristic for this purpose.

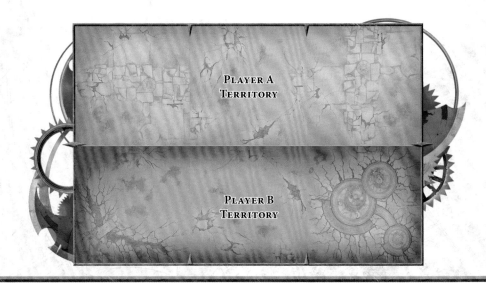

PLAYER A
TERRITORY

PLAYER B
TERRITORY

NARRATIVE PLAY GAMES

With a cast of indomitable heroes and fearsome villains, plots of conquest, zealous loyalty and ruthless betrayal, and a near-endless array of spectacular locations, Warhammer Age of Sigmar is replete with legendary stories. Narrative play is all about re-enacting these epic tales on your own battlefield.

Narrative play games are all about telling stories. This can be as simple as devising a reason for two armies to battle each other, such as a deep-seated rivalry, a contested territory, or a vital objective that must be secured before it falls into the wrong hands. In fact, every time players get together and talk about why their armies might be fighting each other, they are working out a narrative game. This turns a battle into more than just a competitive game to test the generalship of each player, as each battle is weaved into the ongoing story of the Mortal Realms.

Narrative play games can be based on a story or event you have read about in any Warhammer Age of Sigmar publication, or something you have devised yourself after having been inspired by reading about the Mortal Realms. There are endless ways to then build that story into your games. Armies might be modified to better reflect the plot, specific scenery might play a part in recreating the landscape, 'house rules' might be invented to represent the consequences of victory and defeat, and paint schemes can be developed to reflect the forces involved. A game of this type can require more planning to set up than an open or matched play game but, for many, the rewards in terms of immersion and excitement make narrative games well worth the effort. However, if you don't want to spend time crafting a story or making up special rules, there are a number of narrative battleplans available in our books that are based on events that have occurred throughout the history of the Mortal Realms and which are ready to pick up and play straight away.

Because of the vast and varied nature of the Mortal Realms, there is practically no limit to the kind of story you can tell in your games. You can explore objective-based battles in which armies must fight for a vital resource or precious item; scenarios driven by a particular terrain feature, such as a Chaos monolith that seduces wizards with beguiling promises of power; the political tensions between rival warlords in the same Grand Alliance; attacker-defender situations in which one powerful army invades the territory of another; or you can recreate a pivotal battle from the fabled history of the realms.

By linking together the narrative battles you fight, you can turn a story into a saga in which your army and its leaders are the main protagonists. Subsequent battles will continue or conclude the tale begun in the first – a warlord throws down a would-be usurper, an invasion is defeated, or a lost artefact of great power is recovered. In no time your army will be taking part in an epic legend that will be retold by troubadours and chroniclers the realms over for time immemorial!

NARRATIVE PLAY SPECIAL RULES

An easy way to add flavour to narrative play games is to apply special rules that reflect the nature of the battle you wish to replicate or the narrative you're seeking to forge. In this section, we've included a selection of handy, narrative-driven rules that you can easily bolt on to your games to help you achieve the desired effect.

Special rules – sometimes referred to as house rules – are rules that players have invented themselves, or otherwise repurposed from elsewhere to cover special situations, tactics or abilities that they feel need to be represented in their battle. The addition of a few such rules can do a lot to make a game feel unique and interesting, provided they feel appropriate to the context of the game. As such, these rules are especially suited to narrative play, where they can be used to reinforce the key themes of a battle and provide your game with an extra sense of realism.

On the following pages, you will find a number of optional special rules that you can use to bring your narrative games to life. The only restriction on including them is that they can only be used if both players agree, so be sure to discuss it beforehand, and consider only using them with an opponent that you play games against regularly. Just take care not to get carried away – a couple of special rules can add much to a game, but too many will only bog the game down.

Many of these special rules, such as Avatar of Battle, Regiment of Renown and Sustained Attack, can be applied to both players or to just one of them. If one player has a considerably smaller or weaker army than their opponent, rules such as these can serve as a great way to give them an edge.

Avatar of Battle: *This warrior is infamous for their martial prowess, and is known across the Mortal Realms as a bringer of death. In their wake lies a trail of broken armies, the fragments of those who dared to oppose them. With every new battle, their reputation for slaughter grows.*

In the combat phase, your general can be picked to fight twice.

Bitter Enmity: *Amongst the ranks of the enemy is one whose reputation precedes them – a villain whose oppositional crusades, acts of treachery and sheer bloodthirstiness have earned them the ire of all who face them in battle.*

After set-up is complete, but before the battle begins, pick an enemy **Hero** that is on the battlefield. You can re-roll hit rolls of 1 when friendly units target that **Hero**.

Blood Moon: *When a moon hanging in the firmament of one of the Mortal Realms begins to glow a dull blood red, it is always an ill omen. The lands below become washed in malefic energy, bolstering the resolve of the foul servants of Chaos and renewing the vigour of the morbid legions of the dead.*

Add 1 to the Bravery characteristic of all **Chaos** and **Death** units.

Blood Oath: *Many bitter rivalries exist between the champions of the Mortal Realms. Whether the result of jealously, betrayal or the need to avenge a fallen ally, such vows of hatred lead to bloody encounters on the battlefield.*

After set-up is complete, but before the battle begins, pick a friendly **Hero** and an enemy **Hero**. You can re-roll failed hit rolls for the friendly **Hero** you picked when they target the enemy **Hero** you picked with their melee weapons.

Boggy Ground: *The field of battle is foetid and swamp-like, having been drenched by a divine deluge, the re-routing of a mighty river or the vast blood-flow of those previously slain. Those fighting on the battlefield must wade through the waist-high mire, and contended with sink-holes, mud currents and foul bottom-dwelling creatures.*

Units cannot run unless they are able to fly.

Chaos Ascendant: *Through tears in the veil of reality and corrupted Realmgates, the warping energies of Chaos bleed into the Mortal Realms, feeding the daemonic servants of the Ruinous Powers and sustaining their corporeal existence.*

Ignore modifiers (positive or negative) when making save rolls for **Daemon** units.

Concealed Deployment: *Armies shrouded by magical beams of light and shadow, or divided by a crumbling wall of ice, draw up their lines of battle in secret. Each is trying to gain the upper hand by outmanoeuvring their opponents before the first blood of combat is even drawn.*

Instead of setting up normally, the players must set up their units in secret. There are two ways to best achieve this: either you can rig up an improvised barrier in the middle of the battlefield (a line of Citadel Figure Cases is ideal for this) so that the players can set up their units in secrecy, or each player can draw the location of the units they wish to set up on a map before setting them up accordingly once both players have finished. Units that can be set up off the battlefield (such as a Stormcast Eternals unit being set up in the Celestial Realm), can do so as normal – simply place these units to one side whilst setting up or note down which units are doing so on your map.

Dawn Attack: *The morning sun casts its blinding glare across the battlefield, creating silhouettes of the opposing armies. Perhaps the battle is being waged at the break of day, or it could be that the fiery orb has been raised by some sorcerous method. Those firing on the flanks and from the back lines must contend with this fiery glare while their enemies bear down upon them.*

Subtract 1 from hit rolls for missile weapons that are fired during the first battle round.

Delaying Tactics: *Through subterfuge, ambush or illusory magic, a general may be able to tip the odds in their favour by keeping a portion of the enemy army from reaching the battlefield.*

Before set-up, pick D3 units from your opponent's army. These units must be placed to one side and will arrive later in the battle. At the end of any of their movement phases after the first, your opponent can set up these units anywhere wholly within their territory, wholly within 9" of the battlefield edge and more than 9" from any enemy models.

Divine Intervention: *The gods take great interest in the wars that rage across the Mortal Realms, and will smite those who would dare stand in the way of their designs, whilst laying their blessings upon their most loyal servants.*

In your hero phase, you can either inflict D3 mortal wounds on an enemy unit anywhere on the battlefield, or heal D3 wounds that have been allocated to a friendly model anywhere on the battlefield.

Dwindling Morale: *The horror of war grips the blood-drenched combatants. As the battle continues to grind on, what resolve once existed in the army starts to erode, drained by the sight of the dead piled high, the notable absence of their chosen god or the presence of an overwhelming enemy army. Rank-and-file soldiers succumb to their fears, dropping their weapons before turning and fleeing for their lives, and even the most hardened warrior feels their indomitable spirit crack.*

At the start of the third battle round, reduce the Bravery of all models in your army by 1. At the start of the fourth battle round, reduce the Bravery of all models in your army by 2 rather than 1, and by 3 rather than 1 at the start of the fifth and any subsequent battle rounds.

Eclipse: *The sun that hangs over the battlefield begins to darken, its fiery orb obscured by a wandering celestial body, or perhaps enveloped by some fell entity. Those combatants who find themselves below this wondrous omen must fight in shadow until the sun is once again revealed.*

The following effects apply during each battle round as follows:

1st Battle Round: Subtract 1 from hit rolls for missile weapons that are fired at over half their maximum range this battle round.

2nd Battle Round: Subtract 1 from hit rolls for missile weapons that are fired during this battle round.

3rd Battle Round: Subtract 1 from hit rolls for missile weapons that are fired during this battle round. In addition, the ranges of all command abilities, spells and missile weapons are reduced to 12" during this battle round.

4th Battle Round: Subtract 1 from hit rolls for missile weapons that are fired during this battle round.

5th Battle Round: Subtract 1 from hit rolls for missile weapons that are fired at over half their maximum range this battle round.

6th Battle Round (and beyond): No effect.

Eldritch Mist: *An enchanted haze hangs across the field of war, gathering around trees, battlements and shrines of power. All light and sound is sucked into the mist, as are unwary warriors who stray too close.*

Models are not visible to each other if an imaginary straight line 1mm wide drawn between the closest points of the two models crosses over more than 1" of the base of a terrain feature other than open ground and/or hills. In addition, roll a dice for any model that moves through or onto a terrain feature. On a 1, that model is slain.

Flank Attack: *By order of a cunning commander, or based on their own predatory instincts, a group of warriors has crept round the battle-lines and is ready to launch a devastating attack upon their enemies.*

During set-up, one unit can be picked to launch a flank attack – place it to one side instead of setting it up on the battlefield. At the end of any of their movement phases after the first, the controlling player can set up this unit anywhere that is not within their opponent's territory but that is wholly within 9" of the edge of the battlefield. If the unit does not launch its flank attack before the end of the battle, it is destroyed.

A Gathering of Power: *Such is the pivotal nature of this battle that warlords and wizards have been attracted from far and wide, bringing with them the ancient relics, ensorcelled weapons and divinely blessed tomes of their people.*

After set-up is complete, but before the battle begins, you can generate one extra artefact of power and give it to a friendly **Hero** of your choice. If all of your **Heroes** already have an artefact of power and your general is a **Hero**, your general can be given a second artefact of power.

Gravity Vortex: *At certain points in the Mortal Realms, where lines of power converge or great rituals have taken place, the order of nature itself is thrown into complete disarray. In such places, hardened soldiers are dragged to the ground as if suddenly bearing a crushing weight, while skirmishing warriors and light infantry are borne into the sky on invisible currents of magic.*

For the duration of the battle, subtract 1 from the Movement characteristic of units with a Save characteristic of 4+ or better, and subtract 1 from run and charge rolls made for such units. In addition, for the duration of the battle, units with a Save characteristic of 6+ or '-' can fly, and you can re-roll failed charge rolls for such units.

Fog of War: *Despite the best efforts of tacticians and martial diviners, armies often arrive for battle in a state of disarray. The realms are fraught with hazards that can assail an army during its journey, from violent storms to magical phenomena, from pitch-black nights to spontaneously migrating landmasses. When such an army lines up for battle, they may find their archers squaring off against heavy cavalry, or a vital commander left with only the barest honour guard.*

The players roll off, and the winner decides which territory each side will use. The territories are shown on the map below. The players then alternate setting up units one at a time, starting with the player that won the roll-off to determine territories. Each time they do so, they must first roll a dice: on a 1-5, the unit must be set up wholly within the corresponding zone in their territory as shown on the map below; on a 6, the unit can be set up wholly within any zone in their territory. Regardless of which zone

they are in, all units must be set up so that they are more than 12" from enemy territory.

Continue to set up units in this manner until both players have set up their armies. If one player finishes first, the opposing player can set up the rest of the units in their army, one after another as described above.

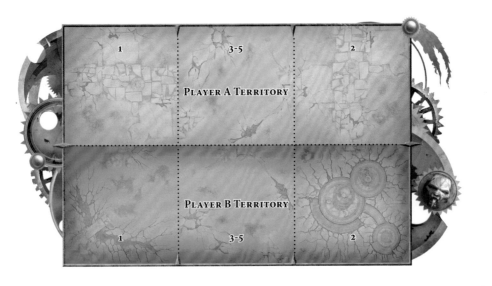

The Great Game: *The influence of the Chaos Gods is in constant flux, with each of the Ruinous Powers waxing and waning in a never-ending cycle. Whichever god is in ascendancy is invariably generous with their gifts.*

At the start of each battle round, each player rolls a dice. Add the score together and consult the table below to see what special rule – if any – applies for the duration of that battle round:

2D6	Result
2-5	No effect.
6	**Boon of Slaanesh:** Units cannot retreat. In addition, no battleshock tests are taken.
7	**Boon of Nurgle:** Roll a dice each time a wound or mortal wound is allocated to one of your models, adding 1 if the model being rolled for is a **Hero**. On a 6+, the wound is negated.
8	**Boon of Khorne:** Add 1 to all charge rolls. In addition, re-roll failed wound rolls of 1 when attacking with melee weapons.
9	**Boon of Tzeentch:** Add 2 to casting rolls.
10-12	No effect.

Illusory Landscape: *Though there are manifold mountain ranges, verdant forests and sprawling cities scattered throughout the Mortal Realms, there are also those landscapes wrought of mere light and shadow, visible for all to behold yet insubstantial as a passing dream.*

Terrain features on this battlefield cannot be garrisoned and are never treated as obstacles. In addition, models can pass across terrain features as if they can fly.

Lifelike Statues: *The hidden relics and sacred sites of the Mortal Realms have many guardians, some of which appear as lifeless statues. But these ominous sentinels may be roused to battle by one who knows the correct incantations or rituals.*

After setting up terrain for the battle, set up as many units as you wish to serve as lifelike statues. These units count as terrain features that are also obstacles, and cannot move or be interacted with in any way unless animated. **Wizards** belonging to one or both players (decide before the battle), know the Gift of Animus spell in addition to any others they know.

Gift of Animus: Gift of Animus has a casting value of 7. If successfully cast, pick a unit of lifelike statues wholly within 18" of the caster. That unit is animated and immediately becomes part of your army, and can act normally from that point on. Once animated, the unit cannot be targeted by the Gift of Animus spell and no longer counts as a terrain feature or an obstacle.

Meteor Shower: *A destructive hail falls from the sky. Whether these meteors are formed of burning rock, crystallized shadow or fragmented realmstone, the effect they have upon those battling on the ground is equally devastating.*

At the start of each battle round, roll a dice. On an even roll, there is no effect. On an odd roll, a meteor shower strikes the battlefield; roll a dice for each unit that is on the battlefield. On a 1, that unit suffers D3 mortal wounds.

Mysterious Omens: *As the constellations traverse the firmament, seers and scryers across the Mortal Realms bear witness to strange portents. Such astral energies can manifest on the battlefield in various ways – a general may experience flashes of unbidden tactical inspiration, or a troupe of fearless warriors may feel an impending sense of dread creeping into their souls.*

Before set-up, roll a dice and consult the table below to see what special rule applies for the duration on the battle:

D6	Result
1	**The Bloodied Crown:** You receive 1 extra command point in each of your hero phases.
2	**The Crimson Aurora:** Subtract 1 from the Bravery characteristic of all units on the battlefield.
3	**The Dark Star:** The maximum range of spells and missile weapons is reduced to 12".
4	**The Absent Flame:** Each time a unit fails a battleshock test, one additional model from that unit flees.
5	**The Veiled Bane:** At the start of your hero phase, roll a dice for each enemy unit on the battlefield. On a 6, that unit suffers 1 mortal wound.
6	**The Void Hearth:** All terrain features have the Deadly scenery rule (see below) in addition to any other scenery rules they may have.

Deadly: Roll a dice for each unit that finishes a normal move or charge move within 1" of any Deadly terrain features. On a 1, that unit suffers D3 mortal wounds.

Necroquake Tremors: *The aftershocks of the Shyish necroquake continue to ripple through the Mortal Realms. Unfettered magical energy and unquiet spirits are released into reality, whereupon they ravage the flesh of the living.*

Roll a dice at the start of each battle round. On a 1, each unit on the battlefield suffers D3 mortal wounds (roll damage separately for each unit), or 1 mortal wound if they are a **Hero**.

Oath of Battle: *Vows of duty, honour and vengeance abound in battle, and those who swear them will continue to fight on, even as the dead bodies of their allies are piled high around them.*

During set-up, pick a friendly unit. That unit does not have to take battleshock tests for the duration of the battle.

Prevailing Winds: *Whether occurring as a natural phenomenon or the result of powerful sorcery, a strong wind blowing behind an army's back is a welcomed ally, sending their missile fire soaring further than before.*

At the start of each battle round, randomly determine one edge of the battlefield. A powerful breeze is blowing from that edge of the battlefield – referred to as the windward edge – in the direction of the opposite edge of the battlefield.

Add 6" to the Range characteristic of a unit's missile weapons when it targets an enemy unit that is further away from the windward edge than the firing unit. Conversely, if the firing unit is further from the windward edge than the target unit, subtract 6" from the Range characteristic of its missile weapons.

Razed Battlefield: *The field of war is wreathed in flames that are the result of a previous battle, fell sorcery or the will of a raging god.*

All terrain features have the Deadly (pg 19) and Burning (see below) scenery rules in addition to any other scenery rules they may have.

Burning: A model cannot see another model if a straight line drawn from the centre of its base to the centre of the other model's base passes across a Burning terrain feature other than open ground and/or hills.

Regiment of Renown: *Through valorous battle or duplicitous deeds, veteran warriors become exemplars of warfare.*

During set-up, pick a friendly unit other than a **Hero** or **Monster**. Add 2 to that unit's Bravery characteristic. In addition, you can re-roll hit rolls of 1 for attacks made by that unit.

Reinforcements: *A canny general will often hold a portion of their army away from the front lines, bringing them forth to battle only when they can cause the greatest harm to the enemy force.*

During set-up, any number of units from your army can be placed to one side as reinforcements; these units will arrive later in the battle. At the end of any of your movement phases after the first, you can set up these units anywhere wholly within your territory, wholly within 9" of any battlefield edge more than 9" from any enemy models.

Designer's Note: *If you wish, the units selected as reinforcements in this manner can represent the arrival of a new army. You can use the Coalition of Death rules from the* Warhammer Age of Sigmar Core Book *to determine how this new army functions – treat both of your armies as belonging to a coalition.*

Stormcast Eternals
Vanguard-Raptor with longstrike crossbow and Aetherwing

Rising Star: *Amongst the champions and renowned spellcasters of the Mortal Realms are those who are rightly revered for their deadly skill or masterful leadership.*

After set-up is complete, but before the battle begins, pick a **Hero** in your army. The model you pick cannot be a named character. Choose a discipline for that **Hero** from the following: Battlefield Strategy, Heroism, Leadership or Martial Prowess. Depending on your choice of discipline, the following special rule applies to that **Hero** for the duration of the battle:

- **Battlefield Strategy:** You receive 1 extra command point at the start of each of your hero phases whilst the **Hero** is on the battlefield.

- **Heroism:** Each time the **Hero** piles in, but before it attacks, add 1 to the Attacks characteristic of their melee weapons (but not their mount's) for each enemy **Hero** within 6" of them. This bonus lasts until the end of that phase.

- **Leadership:** Friendly units within 12" of the **Hero** at the start of the battleshock phase can use the **Hero**'s Bravery characteristic when taking battleshock tests.

- **Martial Prowess:** You can re-roll failed hit rolls for attacks made by the **Hero** (but not their mount).

Saturated with Magic: *There are many sites of power throughout the Mortal Realms. Some of these result from naturally occurring realm magic coalescing within an area, whereas others were formed after apocalyptic arcane battles or fell rituals that went disastrously awry.*

All terrain features have the Arcane scenery rule (see below) in addition to any other scenery rules they may have.

Arcane: Add 1 to casting or unbinding rolls for **Wizards** while they are within 1" of any Arcane terrain features.

Seismic Upheaval: *Whether on a vast volcanic continent or a floating isle of ice, subterranean tremors can have cataclysmic effects on a battlefield.*

At the start of each battle round, roll a dice for each terrain feature on the battlefield. On a 1, it collapses. Collapsed terrain features lose any scenery rules they had and can no longer be garrisoned. They are treated as obstacles for the rest of the battle. Units garrisoning a terrain feature when it collapses suffer 2D6 mortal wounds, and must attempt to leave the terrain feature during the controlling player's movement phase of that battle round. If they are unable to do so, the unit is destroyed.

Sheer Edge: *Battles are not always fought on open planes, with many raging atop the walls of impossibly vast fortresses or on the precipices of yawning chasms.*

Choose or randomly determine an edge of the battlefield to represent a sheer drop or cliff edge. Units cannot move on or off the battlefield via that edge of the battlefield (using abilities such as the Realm Wanderers battle trait, pg 118) unless they can fly. Similarly, units cannot be set up within x" of that battlefield edge using rules such as Reinforcements (see opposite) unless they can fly.

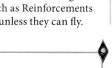

Designer's Note: *This special rule works well to represent an army that has been cornered and forced to fight – simply choose the edge of the battlefield behind the cornered army to be the sheer edge. If you wish to represent a battle being fought in a narrow gorge or atop a plateaux, just apply this special rule to both of the edges of the battlefield that flank the two armies.*

Site of Power: *This battle converges on a site redolent with energy. Perhaps it is a locus of sorcerous power, or a holy site dedicated to the gods of a powerful pantheon.*

When you set up terrain, place one terrain feature (preferably a suitably grand and imposing one) as close as possible to the centre of the battlefield to represent the site of power. This terrain feature has the Nexus of Power scenery rule (see below) in addition to any other scenery rules it may have.

Nexus of Power: Add 1 to casting and unbinding rolls for **Wizards** while they are within 1" of this terrain feature, and add 1 to prayer rolls for **Priests** while they are within 1" of this terrain feature. In addition, add 2 to the Bravery characteristic of units while they are within 6" of this terrain feature.

Skirmish Order: *It is not only apocalyptic battles that shape the fates of the Mortal Realms. Small skirmishing forces may clash over a contested mountain pass or to secure a powerful relic, with the victorious general achieving far more for the larger war effort than the numbers of their force would suggest.*

Players can field no more than five units per army, and must use the minimum size as specified on each unit's warscroll or Pitched Battle profile. In the former case, for example, if a unit's warscroll states that it has '10 or more models', the unit cannot include more than 10 models. Additionally, each player can only include one **Monster** in their army.

Storm of Magic: *A swirling tempest of energy envelops the battlefield. Spellweavers who ply their craft in these conditions find their internal reservoirs of magic greatly bolstered. However, such powerful arcane eddies are perilous, and can consume a caster's life-force in an instant.*

Add 1 to casting rolls. In addition, if a double is rolled for a casting roll, the spell is automatically cast and cannot be unbound, but the caster suffers D3 mortal wounds after the spell's effects have been resolved.

Stormy Weather: *The best-laid battle plans can be cast into disarray by the gathering of dark clouds above the field of war. Whether formed of ice-cold sleet or piping hot blood, a torrent of rain can transform the ground beneath soldiers' feet into a swampy bog, and can soak the bow strings and powder stores of ranged troops huddling on the back lines.*

Roll a dice at the start of each battle round. On a 1, subtract 1 from hit rolls for missile weapons when fired during that battle round, and subtract 1 from run and charge rolls made for units during that battle round.

Sustained Attack: *Some engagements are so brutal that it seems the carnage will never end. As ranked-up troops are cut down and hacked apart, more warriors race in to take their place, trampling over the dead as they press ever onward into their enemy. Such battles often rage for days, leaving only fields of corpses to memorialise the dead.*

Each time a unit other than a **Hero** or **Monster** is destroyed, place it to one side. At the end of any of their following movement phases, the controlling player can roll a dice for each unit that has been placed to one side in this manner: on a 3+, the unit being rolled for can be set up as a new unit anywhere wholly within their territory, wholly within 9" of the edge of the battlefield and more than 9" from any enemy models.

Unstable Ground: *The battlefield is riven with cracks and crumbling features that threaten to buckle at any moment, sending the armies plummeting to a horrible demise. Perhaps combat is raging across a bridge of interwoven crystals that is beginning to fracture under the weight of war, or over a wide sheet of ice beneath which flow deathly cold waters.*

Roll a dice at the start of each player's turn and consult the map below. The number you roll indicates which part of the battlefield is most unstable at that time. At the end of that player's movement phase, roll a dice for each unit that is even partially within that part of the battlefield: on a 1, the unit being rolled for suffers D3 mortal wounds.

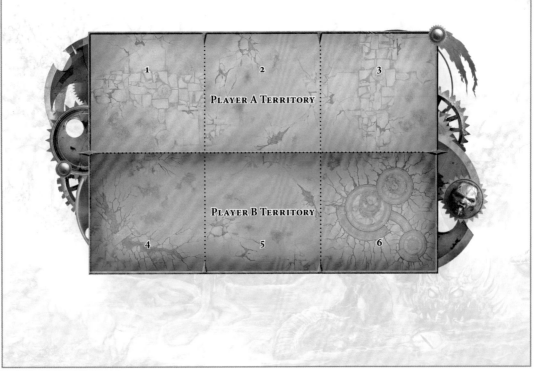

Tunnel Network: *Many battlefields are laced with networks of concealed passages. These may have been constructed by sappers or burrowed by some fell beast, or they may consist of eldritch corridors that wend through the corporeal features of the area.*

All terrain features have the Labyrinthine Tunnels scenery rule (see below) in addition to any other scenery rules they may have.

Labyrinthine Tunnels: If a unit is wholly within 6" of a terrain feature with this scenery rule at the start of your movement phase, you can remove the unit from the battlefield, and then set it up wholly within 6" of another terrain feature with this scenery rule and more than 9" from any enemy models. This counts as that unit's move for that movement phase.

Vagaries of Battle: *Even the most skilled tacticians cannot control every aspect of battle, and a combat may rage well beyond the point that their army can endure. Similarly, a grand assault could be cut short by the swift shroud of night, a furiously raging storm or the interdiction of a malefic force.*

At the end of the third battle round, roll a dice: on a 2+, the battle continues, otherwise the battle ends. If the battle continues, then at the end of the fourth battle round, roll a dice: on a 4+, the battle continues, otherwise the battle ends. The battle automatically ends at the end of the fifth battle round.

Wandering Monsters: *When two armies meet in battle, they are often joined by the gargantuan creatures that inhabit the Mortal Realms. Sometimes these monsters are lured to the battlefield by a nefarious wizard or a canny general, while other times the clashing forces merely spill so much blood that they draw the titanic predators to the theatre of war. Whatever the case, such monsters will unleash devastation upon whoever they encounter – but if their incredible strength and ferocity can be harnessed, they can tip the scales of victory.*

When you set up terrain, set up as many **Monsters** as you wish to serve as wandering monsters. A wandering monster counts as an enemy unit to both sides, but will not move or attack unless a unit moves within 3" of it. At the end of the combat phase, a wandering monster will fight the nearest unit within 3" of it (the controlling player's opponent should roll for these attacks). If two units are equidistant, randomly determine which unit the wandering monster will attack.

Wizards belonging to one or both players (decide before the battle), know the Bind Creature spell in addition to any others they know.

Bind Creature: Bind Creature has a casting value of 6. If successfully cast, pick a wandering monster within 12" of the caster. That unit immediately becomes part of your army, and can act normally from that point on. However, even if you have bound a wandering monster to your army in this manner, the effect is not necessarily permanent; if your opponent successfully casts this spell on a wandering monster that has joined your army, it will immediately switch sides and join your opponent's army instead.

Wild Magic: *Since the shock waves of the Shyish necroquake tore through the Mortal Realms, destructive and undying magic has roamed far and free. Though these endless spells can be hunted and dispelled, in certain areas of power they prove far more resilient than usual.*

Subtract 2 from attempts to unbind or dispel endless spells.

Wrath of the Gods: *Even those battles that seem inconsequential in the grand scheme of the Mortal Realms may be observed by gods, both malign and magnanimous. Should the events unfolding in the thick of combat prove troubling to these gods, they can show their displeasure by smiting the battlefield.*

Each time the roll-off to see which player takes the first turn in each battle round is a tie, make a note. If the roll is tied once before the turn order is resolved, the player that has the second turn in that battle round can pick an enemy unit anywhere on the battlefield to suffer D3 mortal wounds.

If the roll is tied twice before the turn order is resolved, the player that has the first turn in that battle round can pick an enemy unit anywhere on the battlefield to suffer D3 mortal wounds.

Alternate between the players in this manner for any further tied roll-offs at the start of that battle round. The same unit cannot be picked as the target of mortal wounds caused by this special rule until all other units in the same army have been picked once.

HISTORICAL BATTLES

Tales from the Age of Sigmar are filled with heroic deeds and legendary battles. With a little imagination you can recreate these battles with your armies on the tabletop and find out if history will repeat itself, or if your command can alter the course of fate.

The Mortal Realms are rich with legend, with events of great magnitude casting their shadows long over the aeons that follow, storied heroes rising at moments of strife to wrest power from the forces of Chaos, and figures of darkness manipulating fate to serve their own agendas. This vast and ever-unfolding tapestry of history is a mine of inspiration for your narrative games.

You can find exciting tales in any of our publications, from campaign books to Black Library novels. You might find a whole chapter dedicated to a battle you want to recreate in your games, or it might be just a brief mention in the pages of *White Dwarf* that grabs your attention. Crossed swords on maps mark the sites of past battles, their names receding into legend. Artwork provides a window into the Mortal Realms, offering astounding details that can be translated to tabletop games. The annals of the Age of Sigmar are filled with such material, a treasure trove of clashes between great armies, and the meeting of gods, heroes and monsters in battle.

Daemons of Nurgle
Plagueridden

Recreating the legendary battles from the history of the Mortal Realms is, for many, the pinnacle of narrative gaming. Fashioning rules that recreate the circumstances of such a monumental clash can be a truly satisfying exercise, and collecting and painting the fabled heroes and armies that fought in it is, for many, a hugely rewarding project.

Furthermore, the epic grandeur of these events makes for a really thrilling game, imbued with all the gravitas of these epoch-defining moments. However, in your games things might not unravel in the same way as history tells it – the hand of fate might intervene, reversing the fortunes of all involved, or your own strategic skills could turn the tide of battle at the last. Many players enjoy challenging history in this way, determining how they would fare in the shoes of the heroes and warlords that feature in these stories.

There are a number of ways you can recreate a story from the Mortal Realms. Often there will be a battleplan that accompanies the story that you can play right away. Other times you may need to adapt a similar battleplan or create a new one. There is no right or wrong method for doing this, as long as all players agree beforehand. If you want to recreate an event accurately, this involves doing some research to learn the details of the battle, such as the size, disposition and appearance of the armies, which notable heroes were present, where the battle took place and how long it raged for. The narrative play special rules on pages 16-23 can be used to create bespoke narrative battleplans, adding depth and uniqueness to the battlefield stories you tell. Just pick one or two rules that fit in with the story you want to tell. Alternatively, you can use these as inspiration to write your own rules, perfectly suited to the narrative you have chosen.

You can spend time tailoring your collection of Citadel Miniatures to represent a particular army at a particular period in time, taking them through each of the milestone battles that moulded their fate. You can take pains to ensure the terrain matches the description of the region in which each battle took place, representing as best you can that fabled site. Ultimately, the more details you discover or create about the armies, terrain, strategies and special circumstances that were involved, the more enjoyable your historical battles will be. Designing rules, army lists and a modelled battlefield is all part of the fun.

On the following pages are examples of two historical battles that you can play through, or use as inspiration for your own games. The first recreates the battle for the Cascading Path, in which the Oakenbrow Sylvaneth strode out to purge the foul servants of Nurgle from the magical causeway connecting Alarielle's lands. The setting for this battle is based on 'Old Alliances', from The Endless Cycle section in *Battletome: Sylvaneth*, and uses some of the special rules from pages 16-23 to bring the battle to life.

The second historical battle represents the War in the Glymmsforge Catacombs, in which the Stormcast Eternals fought to drive back the invading Death armies led by Nagash, in the hopes of restoring the arcane defences around their city.

For each of these battles, you will find a story describing the setting and armies involved, a battle report detailing the aspects of the story we wanted the rules to reflect, and a finished battleplan that you can play, or adapt for your own narrative games.

THE ROT ENCROACHES

In the Age of Chaos, the servants of Nurgle ravaged the Realm of Life. Great hordes of feculent daemons burst forth from corrupted Realmgates to infect the verdant fields and lush forests of Ghyran. Ancient, city-sized trees that had stood since before the coming of Sigmar were seized by rot, their boughs enveloped in daemonic fungoid growths, and mellifluous mountains withered and died, their floral peaks reduced to diseased compost. As Nurgle's influence spread, his mortal followers also grew in number, and with filth-encrusted blades they slaughtered the inhabitants of this once-thriving realm.

Yet one domain that managed to stave off the worst of the Chaos invasions was the Cascading Path – a magical causeway that wended through Ghyran. Life energy continued to flow through the Cascading Path, and it was on torrents of such magic that the awakening Wargroves of the Sylvaneth were borne throughout the Jade Kingdoms. This network of vitality was an affront to the Father of Plagues, like a vibrant rose persisting amidst a tangle of choking weeds, and Nurgle sought to extend his seeping virulence into these sacred channels.

Nurgle sent forth the Great Unclean One Gloebius the Tidebringer – a gargantuan daemon who had proven to be a rapacious infester. His task was to assault the Druidian Realmgate, a portal that led into the Cascading Path. Gloebius summoned the horde of daemons and rotting mortal warriors known as the Poxfang Tide. These foul servants of the Plague Father had already flooded Ghyran with many diseases, including the Poxfang's Bite – an infection that caused fistulas in the shape of bite marks to bore through the host's body. This hideous affliction had been responsible for completely eradicating the Wanderer tribes of the Mistral Peaks. Now Gloebius and the Poxfang Tide marched on the Forest of Druidia, intent on taking their horrendous ailments through the Realmgate that lay within, and corrupting the Cascading Path beyond.

As the noisome horde marched through the forest, the fertile soil ahead of them began to fester, becoming a bog of putrid fluids. This corruption bled down into the fabric of the realm, afflicting the deepest roots of the most sacred trees, and curdling the life energy that flowed into the Druidian Realmgate. Feeling the effects of this despoilment, several Sylvaneth Wargroves travelled to the forest, including clans from the Dreadwood, Ironbark and Oakenbrow Glades. Together they wove protective spells to ward off the Poxfang's infections, and summoned a mystical fog to slow their enemy's advance.

The defence of the Forest of Druidia was long and harrowing, and many battles were fought. An Ironbark contingent made a stand in the Flutterveldt Clearing only to be subsumed by the daemonic swamp that formed beneath their feet. Those few that crawled out were hacked apart as the Poxfang Tide swept swiftly over them. The warriors of Dreadwood Glade fared only slightly better, butchering a bloated force of Putrid Blightkings that emerged from the depths of the Briarwarrens – but this proved to be a diversionary tactic by Gloebius, who sought to divide the defenders while he himself surged directly towards the heart of the forest.

It was the Sylvaneth of Oakenbrow who made the final stand against the Poxfang Tide at the entrance to the Druidian Realmgate. The lithe warriors were led by the Treelord Ancient Yvenlief, who with talon and branch shredded the foetid invaders by the score. The servants of Nurgle continued to press towards the Realmgate, driven by the promise of bountiful life energy that they could corrupt, but the spirit of the Poxfang Tide was broken when their flabsome general Gloebius was enveloped by the enchanted mist the Sylvaneth had summoned, and vanished from the battlefield. The leaderless Nurgle horde were slaughtered before they could breach the Realmgate, though not before infecting Yvenlief with their deadly rot. In this way, the Poxfang Tide left a permanent scar on the Oakenbrow Glade.

BATTLE FOR THE CASCADING PATH

Inspired by the defence of the Druidian Realmgate by the noble warriors of Oakenbrow, the Battle for the Cascading Path pits an army of Sylvaneth against a festering horde of Nurgle's followers. Using just a few narrative play special rules, this battleplan faithfully represents that fateful engagement, allowing you to recreate the gritty engagement as it happened, or rewrite the course of history completely.

1. THE ROTTED FOREST
The Nurgle hordes have flooded through the Forest of Druidia, spreading disease and decomposition as they go. The once-lush forest is now corrupted beyond recognition, its verdant groves reduced to festering cesspools and its most ancient trees riddled with all manner of daemonic growths. The forest of Druidia is represented by several Sylvaneth Wyldwoods.

2. THE POXFANG TIDE
The ranks of the Poxfang Tide are swollen with rotting daemons and plague-riddled mortal warriors. They are led by Gloebius the Tidebringer, a grotesque Great Unclean One renowned for his fecundity. The Poxfang Tide are heralded by all manner of diseases, most notably the Poxfang's Bite, which ravenously chews through the living matter of those infected.

3. A PESTILENT SWAMP
The Poxfang Tide's feculent corruptions spread before them, transforming the loam of the forest into a mucosal quagmire. While the servants of Nurgle happily frolic through this filth, the malevolent swamp water clings to the limbs of the Sylvaneth warriors, slowing them to a crawl as they wade through the muck. The Boggy Ground special rule (pg 16) represents this battlefield quirk, and we have modified it so that it only applies to the Sylvaneth army.

4. OAKENBROW

A clan from the Sylvaneth Glade of Oakenbrow stands defiantly against the oncoming Nurgle forces. Others of their ilk have already succumbed to the grotesque atrocities of the Poxfang Tide, and the Oakenbrow know that they are all that stands between the enemy and the Cascading Path. The Treelord Ancient Yvenlief leads this clan, and he and his Sylvaneth are prepared to die to halt the spreading daemonic infection.

5. THE VANISHING MIST

Sylvaneth from multiple glades converge upon the Forest of Druidia, and by combining their arcane might they are able to summon an enchanted fog to confuse and confound their foe. This mist hangs thick around the trees and rocks of the forest, allowing the Sylvaneth to move unseen around the battlefield, and even spiriting away those invaders who stray too close to the billowing clouds of magic. We have used the Eldritch Mist special rule (pg 17) to represent this magical fog.

6. THE DRUDIAN REALMGATE

The portal that the Sylvaneth of Oakenbrow are defending leads to the Cascading Path, the network of magical channels and tributaries that criss-crosses the Realm of Life. If the servants of Nurgle are allowed to infest this domain, then their disease will spread with even greater rapidity through Ghyran. The Druidian Realmgate is represented on the battlefield by a Baleful Realmgate model.

FOR THE CASCADING PATH

The Druidian Realmgate that leads to the Cascading Path stands in the middle of the Forest of Druidia in Ghyran. But the once-verdant landscape has been transformed into a festering bog by the creeping advance of the Poxfang Tide, a Nurglesque horde that seeks to corrupt the torrents of life energy flowing through Alarielle's magical causeway. The fertile loam surrounding the Realmgate is now a stagnant swamp, into which the Sylvaneth warriors are slowing sinking. Yet the defenders of the Cascading Path have employed their own magic – a thick, mystical fog that clings to the trees, befuddling the movements of the invaders and spiriting away those foes who wander too deeply into the mist.

THE ARMIES
Each player picks an army as described in the core rules. One player is the Sylvaneth player and their opponent is the Maggotkin player.

The Sylvaneth player should pick an army with the SYLVANETH allegiance and, if they have a suitable model in their collection, include a TREELORD ANCIENT (representing Yvenlief) to be their general.

The Maggotkin player should pick an army with the NURGLE allegiance and, if they have a suitable model in their collection, include a GREAT UNCLEAN ONE from the Great Unclean One warscroll (representing Gloebius the Tidebringer) to be their general.

THE BATTLEFIELD
The Sylvaneth player must first set up a BALEFUL REALMGATE anywhere wholly within their territory, representing the Druidian Realmgate. The players then set up any remaining terrain as described in the core rules.

The battle is being fought in a Nurgle-tainted quagmire surrounding a Realmgate long thought hidden from prying eyes. Copses of SYLVANETH WYLDWOODS should litter the battlefield.

SET-UP
The Sylvaneth player sets up their army first, followed by the Maggotkin player. Units must be set up wholly within their own territory. The Maggotkin player can choose who has the first turn in the first battle round.

BOGGY GROUND
Units belonging to the Sylvaneth player cannot run unless they are able to fly.

ELDRITCH MIST
Models are not visible to models from the Maggotkin player's army if an imaginary straight line 1mm wide drawn between the closest points of the two models crosses over more than 1" of the base of a terrain feature other than open ground and/or hills. In addition, roll a dice for any model from the Maggotkin player's army that moves through or onto a terrain feature. On a 1, that model is slain.

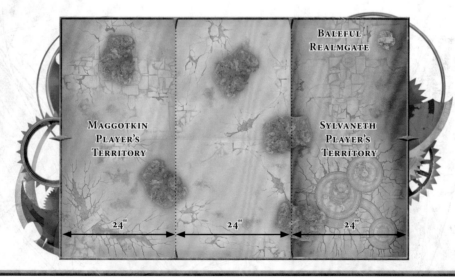

THROUGH THE REALMGATE

At the start of any of their movement phases, the Maggotkin player can remove any friendly units that are wholly within 6" of the **Baleful Realmgate** representing the Druidian Realmgate from the battlefield – they have passed through the Realmgate and into the Cascading Path beyond. Units that pass through the Realmgate in this manner take no further part in the battle, but count towards the victory conditions (see right).

GLORIOUS VICTORY

The level of victory is determined by the number of units from the Maggotkin player's army (if any) that have passed through the Realmgate (see below) before the end of the fifth battle round:

No. of units	Result
0	**Major victory** to the Sylvaneth player.
1	**Minor victory** to the Sylvaneth player.
2	**Minor victory** to the Maggotkin player.
3+	**Major victory** to the Maggotkin player.

A CITY AMONGST THE DEAD

In Shyish, the mighty city of Glymmsforge was built around the Shimmergate. This ancient Realmgate connects the Realm of Death to the Realm of Heavens, and vast concentric walls were constructed around it to hold back even the mightiest of mortal armies. Yet there were other enemies that threatened Glymmsforge – the daemonic servants of the Chaos Gods, and the ethereal legions of the Great Necromancer Nagash.

Since before Sigmar's coming, the Shimmergate stood at the heart of Lyria, an underworld in which the dead were given respite from strife for their pure and noble deeds in life. The city of Glymmsforge that arose around it was constructed by Dispossessed masons, and bore the sturdiness inherent in the works of the duardin. Yet even these defences did not make the Shimmergate impervious to invasion. Slaanesh-worshipping tribes sought to corrupt the Realmgate and gain passage into Azyr, but the Anvils of the Heldenhammer scoured them from the land, fortifying Glymmsforge and establishing a vassal Stormkeep at the city's heart. Over the years, duardin, aelf and man worked together to reinforce Glymmsforge, erecting layers of walls that extended the city's perimeter. Though these walls made a mockery of invading armies, they could not hold back the malicious spirits that pervaded Shyish. Countless inhabitants of Glymmsforge were abducted in the night, pulled from their beds by spectral claws, or cut down in the darkness by flights of unquiet gheists. The city required protection not just from the living, but from the dead.

Defence against the ethereal terrors came when the remains of twelve Celestial Saints were brought to Glymmsforge from the Realm of Heavens. So redolent with Azyrite energy were these hallowed remains that their mere presence warded against daemons and the undead, driving such foul entities back as though the God-King himself had levelled his will against them.

Each of the twelve saints was interred in mausoleums around the city, forming the extremities of a twelve-pointed star. The star itself was encircled by a channel of blessed silver from Chamon, into which was ground sacred salts of purple hue. Thus the outer boundary of Glymmsforge was sanctified, and rendered impassable to the fell enemies of Sigmar – but even this perimeter would not hold forever.

THE FIRST SIEGE OF GLYMMSFORGE

The undead queen Lady Olynder desired to add the city of Glymmsforge to her Kingdom of Grief. A skeletal army marched upon the city, led by Vaslbad the Unrelenting, a vampiric general whose dark banner protected him from any magic that could harm his undying form. The Anvils of the Heldenhammer, alongside the Free People of Glymmsforge, lined the walls and prepared to defend the city against the morbid invaders.

Many died in the defence of Glymmsforge, yet the siege was eventually broken. During an assault on the northern mausoleum gate, the Prosecutor-Prime Galen Sleekwing flew out to meet the approaching enemy general, and the winged Stormcast Eternal tore the malefic banner from Vaslbad's hand. Left without magical protection, Vaslbad was impaled by Knossian Glymm – a descendant of the royal family that had held kingship over Glymmsforge since the Age of Myth. Glymm himself was cut down by the spiteful last lunge of the vampire general, but as he lay dying he was claimed by Sigmar, ascending to the Heavens on a beam of cerulean light. There he was reforged as Knossus Heavensen, Lord-Arcanum of a Sacrosanct Chamber.

In another tale of glory, the spellshaper Serafin Heldett led several Free People companies in the gruelling battle for the city's western gate. There they fought an unending horde of Deadwalkers, whose numbers were bolstered by every defender that was slain. For nine days her troops held back the dead, and with the help of the city's Eldritch Council, Heldett summoned arcane sandstorms that tore the decrepit flesh from the enemy army. On the last day the spellshaper turned her magical wrath on the Necromancers who had steered the Deadwalker horde, immolating them with arcane fire before she herself was felled by an eldritch bolt. She too was snatched away by Sigmar and reforged as the Knight-Incantor Zeraphina Heldensdottor. Yet not every defender of Glymmsforge had such a glorious end.

It was the veteran soldier Vorgen Malendrek who defended the city's southern gate. There he used his considerable experience and strategic wit to outmanoeuvre the undead thrall known as the Slender Knight. By baiting the Slender Knight's ghastly horsemen into a series of traps, Malendrek whittled down the enemy. The victory he won that day was earned through blood, yet despite his cunning and unflagging determination, Malendrek was not singled out by Sigmar to be reforged as one of the God-King's eternal warriors. In the grand scheme of things, Malendrek's efforts were barely even noticed.

By the time the siege was finally broken, Malendrek had sustained a number of injuries – to his body, to his pride and to his soul. A growing bitterness festered inside the veteran, causing him to withdraw ever more into reclusion. In his solitude he began to hear insidious whispers, the voice of a mythical wizard-king whose true name had been forgotten. This voice instilled Malendrek with twisted hope, promising him a position at the head of an army – a position that he had earned through his deeds. There was but one more task required of the suffering veteran before he could receive his due. The voice told him to dig up a section of the sacred perimeter encircling the city, to remove a small portion of

the blessed salt, and replace it with mundane purple sand. For a time Malendrek ignored this notion, but the whispering voice in his mind grew ever more persistent, until, on the anniversary of the victory over Vaslbad, his embittered spirit could take no more. He rode to the outskirts of Glymmsforge to do as he was bid, and in that moment he gave himself to Nagash.

THE SECOND SIEGE OF GLYMMSFORGE

When the city of Glymmsforge once again came under attack from the undead, it was Malendrek who rode at the head of the hordes. The promise of the voice had been fulfilled – he was the general of an army, a leader of gheists and wraiths – and Malendrek had himself been transformed into a spectre, his hollow eye sockets glowing with baleful flame. With his ethereal army behind him, the traitor general crossed the hallowed threshold into Glymmsforge, through the breach that he himself had created in his final living moments.

But Sigmar was not caught off-guard by this insidious ploy. With the cataclysmic effects of the Shyish necroquake being felt throughout the Mortal Realms, the God-King had sent out warriors from his Sacrosanct Chambers to prepare for whatever dread events were to unfold. When Malendrek and his undead army rode to the southern gate at Glymmsforge, they were greeted by a host of Stormcast Eternals, amongst whom were two old allies of the traitor veteran – Knossus Heavensen and Zeraphina Heldensdottor.

The undead army smashed into the line of Stormcast Eternals, spectral claws tearing through armour and blessed hammers reducing the attackers to motes of spirit energy. As this battle raged, a call came from the defenders of the south-western gate, the tomb-site of the redeemed gargant Templesen. A portion of Malendrek's force, led by the Lord Executioner Keranus,

was despoiling the mausoleum of this Celestial Saint, shattering the wards emanating from the hallowed ground and threatening to further subvert the sacred wards that protected Glymmsforge. Knossus Heavensen recognised the peril facing the city. Not only was the enchanted perimeter dangerously close to being unbound, but if fell death magic could be used to resurrect the mighty gargant Templesen, then the defenders would be faced with a truly monstrous siege creature. Unable to leave the battle-lines at the southern gate, Heavensen sent his greatest lieutenant – the Knight-Incantor Zeraphina Heldensdottor – to reclaim the Tomb of the Redeemed from the spirit horde.

Despite a heavy toll in casualties, Heldensdottor's retinue were able to slaughter the cabal of Necromancers who were weaving a hex over the mausoleum. But it quickly became apparent that whilst the blessed circle around Glymmsforge remained broken, the city would never be safe from the legions of the Great Necromancer. The sacred sand that had been defiled by Malendrek had to be restored, but the nearest deposits of this substance lay outside the city, in the catacombs claimed by the armies of the dead.

It was then that the skies rumbled with thunder, and the Celestant-Prime manifested in Glymmsforge. The Avenging Angel of Azyr took what forces could be spared and pushed out through the eastern front, fighting towards the Gate Sinister, a Realmgate that led to the catacombs where the sacred salt was interred. Upon traversing the portal, Sigmar's warriors found an enormous horde of undead awaiting them, and the cerulean energies surrounding the Celestant-Prime crackled as he readied his forces for battle. But a chill air dampened even his heavenly spirit, for something was coming to the catacombs, a deathly being of immense power – Nagash himself…

WAR IN THE GLYMMSFORGE CATACOMBS

The Hammers of Sigmar, led by the Celestant-Prime, have struck deep into Nagash's realm to combine forces with the Anvils of the Heldenhammer outside the city of Glymmsforge. They hope to recover an ossuary of sacred grave salt from the catacombs that have been claimed by Nagash's forces, and use it to restore the city's arcane defences.

1. NAGASH

The forces of Death surrounding the catacombs are quick to warn their master of the arrival of the Stormcast Eternals. As such, the Great Necromancer has begun to manifest himself on the battlefield. The Delaying Tactics special rule (pg 17) ensures that the Death player cannot bring Nagash into the game until after the first battle round, representing the Supreme Lord of the Undead appearing in a massive coalescence of amethyst energy.

2. GUARDIANS OF THE CATACOMBS

The entrance to the catacombs is defended by two Morghast statues. Using the Lifelike Statues special rule (pg 19), the Death player can bring these statues to life and add them to their army.

3. THE LOWER CATACOMBS

The entrance to the lower catacombs is the objective of the Stormcast Eternals' attack, as the ossuary is located inside.

4. GATE SINISTER

The Hammers of Sigmar are using a Realmgate called Gate Sinister to reach the battlefield. This is represented by a Baleful Realmgate model.

5. THE SINISTER UNDERWAY

The upper catacomb peaks are threaded with a network of magical tunnels called the Sinister Underway. With the exception of the entrance to the lower catacombs (see 3.), all of the tunnel entrances on the battlefield are connected using the Tunnel Network special rule (pg 23), and can be traversed by units from either army during their player's movement phase.

7. THE CELESTANT-PRIME

The Stormcast Eternals army is led by the Celestant-Prime.

6. ANVILS OF THE HELDENHAMMER

These noble warriors have been fighting a prolonged campaign to defend the city of Glymmsforge, and march swiftly to aid their comrades. The Sustained Attack special rule (pg 22) represents the Anvils of the Heldenhammer arriving to reinforce the Hammers of Sigmar, and allows the Stormcast Eternals player to bolster their army even as their warriors are slain in battle.

BATTLEPLAN
THE GLYMMSFORGE CATACOMBS

Interred in the catacombs in the Zircona Desert is the sacred sand needed to restore the magical perimeter around the city of Glymmsforge – but the Great Necromancer and his deathly legions stand ready to slaughter the questing Stormcast Eternals.

THE ARMIES
Each player picks an army as described in the core rules. One player is the Stormcast Eternals player and their opponent is the Legions of Nagash player.

The Stormcast Eternals player should pick an army with the **STORMCAST ETERNALS** allegiance and, if they have the model in their collection, include the **CELESTANT-PRIME** to be their general.

The Legions of Nagash player should pick an army with the **GRAND HOST OF NAGASH** allegiance and, if they have the model in their collection, include **NAGASH** to be their general.

THE BATTLEFIELD
The Stormcast Eternals player must first set up a Baleful Realmgate anywhere wholly within their territory, representing the Gate Sinister. The Legions of Nagash player must then set up a suitable terrain feature to represent the lower catacombs entrance. The players then set up any remaining terrain as described in the core rules.

The battle is being fought in the mountainous outskirts of Glymmsforge. Dark tunnels line the rocky crags that loom over a mausoleum at the foot of the valley, and an entrance to the foreboding lower catacombs yawns wide.

LIFELIKE STATUES
After setting up terrain for the battle, the Legions of Nagash player sets up a **MORGHAST** unit as lifelike statues anywhere wholly within their territory. This unit counts as a terrain feature and also an obstacle, and cannot move or be interacted with in any way until animated. All **WIZARDS** belonging to the Legions

of Nagash player know the Gift of Animus spell in addition to any others they know.

Gift of Animus: Gift of Animus has a casting value of 7. If successfully cast, pick a unit of lifelike statues wholly within 18" of the caster. That unit immediately becomes part of your army, and can act normally from that point on. Once animated in this manner, the unit cannot be targeted by the Gift of Animus spell and no longer counts as a terrain feature or an obstacle.

SET-UP
The Legions of Nagash player sets up their army first (with the exception of **NAGASH**), followed by the Stormcast Eternals player (with the exception of the **CELESTANT-PRIME**). Units must be set up wholly within their own territory. The Stormcast Eternals player can choose who has the first turn in the first battle round.

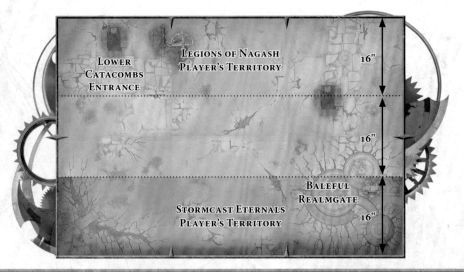

DELAYING TACTICS

Nagash must be placed to one side and will arrive later in the battle. At the end of any of their movement phases after the first, the Legions of Nagash player can set up Nagash anywhere wholly within their territory, wholly within 9" of the battlefield edge and more than 9" from any enemy models.

SUSTAINED ATTACK

Each time a unit other than a **Hero** or **Monster** from the Stormcast Eternals player's army is destroyed, place it to one side. At the end of any of their following movement phases, the Stormcast Eternals player can roll a dice for each unit that has been placed to one side in this manner. On a 3+ the unit being rolled for can be set up as a new unit anywhere wholly within their territory, wholly within 9" of the edge of the battlefield and more than 9" from any enemy models, or anywhere wholly within 6" of the Baleful Realmgate representing the Gate Sinister and more than 9" from any enemy models.

TUNNEL NETWORK

With the exception of the lower catacombs entrance (see map), all terrain features have the Labyrinthine Tunnels scenery rule (see below) in addition to any other scenery rules they may have.

Labyrinthine Tunnels: If a unit is wholly within 6" of a terrain feature with this scenery rule at the start of your movement phase, you can remove the unit from the battlefield, and then set it up wholly within 6" of another terrain feature with this scenery rule and more than 9" from any enemy models. This counts as that unit's move for that movement phase.

GLORIOUS VICTORY

At the end of any battle round in which a unit from the Stormcast Eternals player's army is within 3" of the lower catacombs entrance, roll a dice. On a 4+, they have found the sacred salt. The game ends immediately and the Stormcast Eternals player wins a **major victory**. If, after five battle rounds, the sacred salt has not been found, the Legions of Nagash player wins a **major victory**.

GATHERING OF MIGHT

The stories of the Age of Sigmar often tell of grand, epic battles, where the fate of an entire region of one of the Mortal Realms – sometimes even one of the Realmspheres themselves – hangs in the balance. If you wish to re-enact one of these cataclysmic clashes, perhaps even fielding your entire collection of miniatures when you do so, then the guidelines presented here are for you.

Gathering of Might provides a set of simple modifications to the Warhammer Age of Sigmar core rules that allows a massive game featuring hundreds of models on either side to be played at a faster and more satisfying pace than would normally be possible.

These rules are best suited to big, multi-player games, or grudge matches between two players that each have especially large collections of miniatures at their disposal. The rules that follow are designed for a multi-player game in which two or more players team up, combining their armies into one large force – but you can easily adapt these rules to suit a two-player game.

THE ARMIES
Split the players into two sides, using any method you prefer. The two sides can be made up of different numbers of players. Each of the players then chooses an army as described in the core rules.

Each player commands the models in their army and is allowed to decide what they do, how they move and so on, and they make all of the dice rolls for their own units. All models on the same side are considered to be friendly towards one another.

We recommend that you do not use Pitched Battle points when choosing armies. Unless you have the timeless patience of Nagash himself or are simply a glutton for punishment, writing army lists for games of this size can bog things down before you even get started. As such, we suggest using a faster, simpler approach to balancing the two sides, such as fielding an even number of units.

In addition, the rules for warscroll battalions should not be used in these games, even if the units being fielded qualify for one or more battalions.

Note that this means that neither side will start the battle with any command points.

GENERALS AND WARLORDS
Each player picks a general for their army as normal. You must also pick one player from each side to be the warlord. This is often the player fielding the largest force. If, at any time during the game, the side cannot decide in what order to carry out actions, then the warlord has final say on the order of events.

In addition, if a dice needs to be rolled for the whole team, the warlord makes that dice roll. Finally, any victory conditions from a battleplan that apply to an army general only apply to the warlord's general unless specifically noted otherwise.

THE BATTLEFIELD

Because of the scale of these battles, you may find you need to play on a larger battlefield than normal. As a guideline, we suggest using a 2'x4' battlefield for every 5 units on each side.

SET-UP

Speeding up the set-up process is an important part of fighting a big battle; the sooner set-up is complete, the sooner the fighting can get underway! We suggest using one of the three following methods for a rapid set-up: Secret Bidding, Timed Deployment or Concealed Deployment. In any case, units that can be set up off the battlefield (such as a Stormcast Eternals unit being set up in the Celestial Realm), can do so as normal – simply place these units to one side whilst setting up.

Secret Bidding: Both sides secretly bid (by writing down) the amount of time they want to take setting up. Bids must be in whole minutes. If both sides bid the same amount of time, repeat this process until one side has bid lower. The side that bids lowest sets up their units first, anywhere wholly within their territory, but only has the length of time that they bid to do so. The other side then sets up their units anywhere wholly within their territory, but only has the length of time that they bid to do so. If they feel they have set up a sufficient number of units, each side can choose to finish setting up early. Any units that cannot be set up in time are placed to one side as Reserves (see below).

If one side's bid was twice as long or more than the opposing side's bid, then the players from that side must roll a dice before they set up a unit on the battlefield; on a roll of 1 or 2 that unit must be placed to one side as Reserves (though **HEROES** only have to be made Reserves on a roll of 1).

Timed Deployment: Both sides agree on a single time limit for set-up (we recommend you keep it short!). Both sides then set up their units simultaneously, anywhere wholly within their respective territories, within the agreed time limit. Any units that cannot be set up in time are placed to one side as Reserves (see below). If they feel they have set up a sufficient number of units, each side can choose to finish setting up early.

Concealed Deployment: This works in the same way as the Timed Deployment method, except that the players rig up an improvised barrier in the middle of the battlefield. The sides then set up their units in secrecy.

RESERVES

Reserve units can enter play in any of their side's movement phases starting from the second battle round. The unit must be set up anywhere wholly within their side's territory, wholly within 6" of the battlefield edge and more than 9" from any enemy models. This counts as their move for that movement phase.

FIGHTING THE BATTLE

Instead of each player taking a turn, each side takes a turn. The two warlords roll off against each other to see which side has the first turn each round.

Where individual players would normally alternate taking actions, the sides alternate taking actions, with each player in the team being allowed to carry out their actions.

BATTLE ROUNDS

Play each battle round as normal, but with the following modifications to each phase that simplify and speed up the process.

HERO PHASE – COMMAND POINTS

In the maelstrom of battle, one leader will usually come to the fore. By uniting under this storied warrior's banner, even a large and diverse army can find unity.

Each side generates 3 command points instead of 1 at the start of their hero phase if their warlord's general is on the battlefield.

HERO PHASE – SPELLS

In the largest battles, wizards will often forgo the ability to assail their enemies with a barrage of lesser spells to better focus their attentions on unleashing their most powerful and destructive magic.

Each **Wizard** can only attempt to cast or unbind a single spell in each hero phase. However, if a model would normally be able to cast or unbind more than one spell in each hero phase, the controlling player can instead add 2 to casting and unbinding rolls they make for that model for each spell after the first that they would normally be able to cast or unbind. For example, Ethrac Glott – one of the fabled Glottkin brothers – can normally cast two spells in his hero phase, so would add 2 to his casting roll when attempting to cast a spell; however, Ethrac can only attempt to unbind one spell in each enemy hero phase, so would receive no bonus to his unbinding roll.

SHOOTING PHASE – VOLLEY FIRE

Those armed with missile weapons can fire long, arcing shots at far greater distances if they sufficiently elevate their trajectory, but doing so comes at a cost in accuracy.

Models armed with missile weapons can target enemy units at up to twice their normal range, but subtract 1 from their hit rolls if they do so. However, models cannot target an enemy **Hero** in this manner unless it is a **Monster Hero**.

COMBAT PHASE – MASSED MELEES

As the swirling melee escalates into a bloodbath, casualties mass on both sides at an astonishing rate as attrition takes its terrible toll.

In the combat phase, starting with the side whose turn is taking place, each side takes it in turns to pile in with all of their units that are eligible to do so. Once this is done, players take it in turns to make attacks with all of their units that are eligible to do so. When resolving these attacks, all of the models in the unit are considered to be within range to attack with all of their melee weapons. In addition, attacks made in the combat phase are all resolved simultaneously, meaning that even though one player may attack with their unit first, any enemy models they slay will be able to attack before they are removed as casualties. One thing is certain – combat will always be a bloody affair!

LEGENDARY ABILITIES

In a Gathering of Might battle, each side has access to the following legendary abilities.

LEGENDARY TRAITS

If the warlord's general is a **Hero**, that model can have a legendary trait from the list opposite. Pick the trait that best suits that general's personality or roll a dice to randomly determine a trait. If the warlord must select a new general during a battle, immediately choose or roll a trait for them. Legendary traits have no effect on attacks made by a general's mount unless noted otherwise.

GIFTS OF THE GODS

Each side can have one gift of the gods from the list opposite, which they can use once per battle. Pick the gift that best suits the personality of your side's divine patron or roll a dice to randomly determine the gift your side will receive.

LEGENDARY ARTEFACTS

One **Hero** on each side (chosen by the warlord) can be given a legendary artefact from the list on page 40. Legendary artefacts have no effect on attacks made by a **Hero**'s mount unless noted otherwise.

LEGENDARY SPELLS

All **Wizards** share the knowledge of the legendary spell associated with the Grand Alliance they belong to, regardless of which side they're on. These are listed on page 41. However, each legendary spell can only be successfully cast once in each side's hero phase, regardless of how many **Wizards** the side has. However, if a model fails to cast a legendary spell or the legendary spell is unbound, a different **Wizard** from the same side can attempt to cast that legendary spell in the same phase.

LEGENDARY TRAITS

D6 Result

1 Lord of War: *This general is a tactical genius without equal, and is capable of devising new strategies and countering the ploys of their foes amidst the clangour of battle.*

Whilst this general is on the battlefield, roll a dice each time you spend a command point; on a 5+, that command point is immediately refunded.

2 Refusal to Yield: *Bestowed with a robust constitution and unflagging vigour, this mighty general is able to battle on through wounds that would kill many a lesser warrior.*

Add 3 to this general's Wounds characteristic.

3 Battle Fury: *In the thick of combat, this mighty warlord is a raging storm, striking swiftly to cut through the massed ranks of enemies before them.*

Add 1 to the Attacks characteristic of all of this general's melee weapons (including their mount's).

4 Absolute Authority: *This general holds an unquestioned position of leadership, and they inspire unwavering loyalty and bravery in the warriors who fight beneath their banner.*

Friendly units wholly within 18" of this general at the start of the battleshock phase do not need to take battleshock tests.

5 Taskmaster: *With shouts of inspiration or bellowed threats, this exacting general drives the warriors under their command ever forward.*

Friendly units wholly within 18" of this general at the start of the charge phase can charge even if they ran or retreated earlier in the turn.

6 Crusader: *This warlord fights with fanatical vigour, and serves as an exemplar of righteous fury to the soldiers who follow them into battle.*

Add 1 to hit rolls for friendly units wholly within 18" of this general at the start of the combat phase if this general charged earlier in the turn.

GIFTS OF THE GODS

D6 Result

1 Gift of Healing: *Bones mend and flesh re-knits as restorative energy flows through the divinely chosen champion.*

Use this gift at the start of any phase. Pick a friendly **HERO** or **MONSTER** and heal D6 wounds that have been allocated to that model.

2 Gift of Urgency: *The recipients of this gift are imbued with deific vigour, allowing them to close upon their foes with blinding speed.*

Use this gift after making a charge roll for a friendly unit. Roll a dice and add the result to the unit's charge distance this phase.

3 Gift of Determination: *Those upon whom this blessing is bestowed see the movements of their enemies before they have been made.*

Use this gift in the combat phase, after making hit rolls for a friendly unit. Re-roll hit rolls of 1 for that unit this phase.

4 Gift of New Life: *While the desires of the gods remain unfulfilled, the dead are not guaranteed a respite from battle.*

Use this gift at the start of any phase. Pick a friendly unit and roll a dice; you can return a number of slain models to the unit that have a combined Wounds characteristic equal to or less than the number rolled.

5 Gift of Sorcery: *Arcane power surges through the wizard, bestowing upon them a portion of their patron god's might.*

Use this gift after making a casting attempt with a friendly **WIZARD** (whether or not the attempt was successful). You can immediately attempt to cast another spell, apart from a legendary spell, with that model. The model retains any casting bonuses they may have, and can even attempt to cast the same spell a second time.

6 Gift of Slaughter: *The chosen warriors are filled with divine rage and fall upon their enemies with fanatical brutality.*

Use this gift in the combat phase, before making wound rolls for a friendly unit. Add 1 to wound rolls for that unit this phase.

LEGENDARY ARTEFACTS

D6   Result

1   **Dawnstar Blade:** *This ancient blade is said to have been forged using the first rays of light to have fallen upon the Mortal Realms, and over the uncountable aeons it has lost none of its radiant power.*

Pick one of the bearer's melee weapons. Add 2 to the Attacks characteristic of that weapon, or double the Attacks characteristic of that weapon while your side has a greater number of victory points.

2   **Cloak of Transience:** *Once donned, this ethereal cloak appears to vanish. Only when the wearer is threatened by an incoming blow does the cloak materialise again, becoming more solid and impenetrable than the most robust armour.*

Ignore the attacking weapon's Rend characteristic when making save rolls for the bearer.

3   **Prism of the Everwind:** *Each of the gleaming facets of this lustrous crystal is attuned to the magic of a different realmsphere, allowing powerful sorcerous energies to be bound within and later released.*

After set-up is complete, but before the battle begins, pick one spell from the legendary spells list (pg 41) to be bound within the Prism of the Everwind. Once per battle, in your hero phase, the bearer can cast the spell bound with the Prism, even if they are not a **WIZARD**. If the bearer is a **WIZARD**, they can cast this spell in addition to any spell they can cast normally that phase. Roll a 2D6 to determine the casting roll of the spell for the purposes of any unbinding attempt, but the spell is otherwise cast automatically.

4   **Blade of Last Resort:** *This sentient blade seeks out heroes who are willing to plunge themselves into battle, and it is there that the Blade of Last Resort bestows upon its wielder unparalleled prowess. However, for this burst of deadly power there is a price to pay in blood.*

Pick one of the bearer's melee weapons to be the Blade of Last Resort. You can activate the Blade of Last Resort once per battle, at the start of the combat phase. When you do so, you can re-roll failed hit rolls and wound rolls for that weapon until the end of the phase. In addition, if the weapon has a Damage characteristic of D3 or D6, you can re-roll damage rolls for it until the end of the phase. Finally, the weapon's

Rend characteristic is improved to -5 until the end of the phase. However, after resolving the bearer's attacks, they immediately suffer D6 mortal wounds.

5   **Crown of Command:** *The wearer of this mythical headdress senses every potential outcome of battle before it happens, allowing them to direct their forces with uncanny strategic insight.*

Whilst the bearer is on the battlefield, your side receives an extra D3 command points at the start of each of your hero phases.

6   **Helm of Many Eyes:** *The unblinking eyes that bejewel this helm see into the past and future, and through their prescient visions they bestow upon the wearer a devastating edge against any opponent.*

In the combat phase, pile in and resolve the bearer's attacks before any other units fight. Models slain by the bearer in this manner are removed as casualties immediately and cannot fight later in the phase. If both sides have this item, the side whose turn is taking place can fight with their bearer before the other side's bearer fights.

LEGENDARY SPELLS

ORDER

Enlightenment: *By calling upon the stars in the firmament, a wizard can cause the radiance of Azyr to shine down upon their allies. This light burns away whatever fear may have crept into the spirit of those illuminated. Furthermore, warriors bathed in this light are able divine the skeins of fate as they lock blades with their enemies, allowing them to strike true where their foes least expect.*

ORDER WIZARDS know this legendary spell. Enlightenment has a casting value of 10. If successfully cast, pick a friendly unit that is wholly within 18" of the caster and visible to them. Until the start of your next hero phase, you can re-roll failed hit rolls for that unit and the unit does not need to take battleshock tests.

CHAOS

Oblivion: *By focusing their hatred upon their enemy, the wizard creates a locus through which the obliterative energies of the Dark Gods are able to flow through the veil of reality and into the Mortal Realms. Those caught within this spiteful torrent are often torn limb from limb, or have their bodies twisted into cruel and torturous configurations, before being sucked into the nightmarish Realm of Chaos.*

CHAOS WIZARDS know this legendary spell. Oblivion has a casting value of 10. If successfully cast, pick an enemy unit that is wholly within 18" of the caster and visible to them. Roll a dice for each model in the unit. For each roll of 4+ that unit suffers 1 mortal wound.

DEATH

Malediction of Nagash: *Fingers of necrotic energy extend outward from the caster to envelop their enemies, filling the hearts of those they grasp with a deathly ennui that saps them of their will to fight.*

DEATH WIZARDS know this legendary spell. Malediction of Nagash has a casting value of 10. If successfully cast, pick an enemy unit that is wholly within 18" of the caster and visible to them. Until your next hero phase, subtract 1 from that unit's wound rolls. In addition, in the combat phase, that unit cannot fight until all other eligible units (on either side) have done so, and any models in that unit that were slain earlier that phase cannot attack. If both sides have a unit affected by this spell, the side whose turn is taking place can fight with their affected unit before the other side's unit fights.

DESTRUCTION

Primal Onslaught: *The minds of those upon whom this magic falls are temporarily purged of thought and rationality. Whatever memories and ideals they may once have held are replaced by a raging, primitive urge to fight.*

DESTRUCTION WIZARDS know this legendary spell. Primal Onslaught has a casting value of 10. If successfully cast, pick a friendly unit that is wholly within 18" of the caster and visible to them. In each combat phase until your next hero phase, that unit can fight twice. In addition, if the unit is a **MONSTER**, then until your next hero phase, re-roll hit rolls of 1 for that unit's melee weapons.

BATTLEPLAN
NEXUS OF POWER

Countless wars have been fought for control of this hallowed site, where numerous sacred waylines converge. Kings and warlords are willing to strike up all manner of unlikely bargains and dark pacts in order to form an alliance mighty enough to destroy all others aspiring to claim this vital region.

GATHERING OF MIGHT

This is a Gathering of Might battle for two or more players. Use the Gathering of Might rules from pages 36-41.

THE ARMIES

Each side picks armies as described on page 36.

SET-UP

Choose one of the three set-up methods, as described on page 37. Units must be set up wholly within their side's territory more than 9" from enemy territory.

OBJECTIVES

This battle is fought to control a number of objectives, which varies according to the size of the battlefield being used – specifically 1 objective per 2'x4' of the battlefield. The objectives are located at the centre of each 2'x4' section of the battlefield, as shown on the map. You may wish to show their location with a small marker.

GLORIOUS VICTORY

The side that has scored the most victory points (see below) at the end of the fifth battle round wins a **minor victory**, unless they win by 10 or more victory points in which case they win a **major victory**. If both sides have the same number of victory points, the result is a **draw**.

VICTORY POINTS

Each side scores victory points at the end of each of their turns for each objective they control. The number of victory points is equal to the number of the current battle round. For example, a side that controls 1 objective at the end of their turn in the third battle round scores 3 victory points.

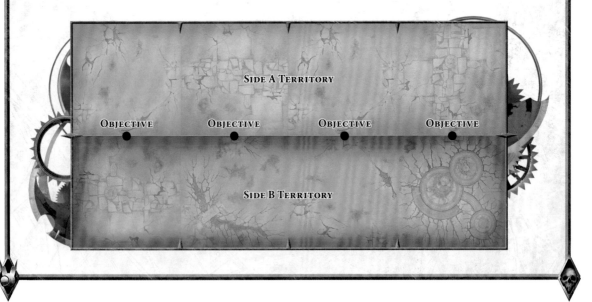

SIDE A TERRITORY

OBJECTIVE   OBJECTIVE   OBJECTIVE   OBJECTIVE

SIDE B TERRITORY

BATTLEPLAN
GRAND SLAUGHTER

Two huge armies have converged to contest control of these lands. Only courage and valour on the battlefield will win the day, only those with the strength to strike down their foes in glorious battle will triumph. Legends are sure to rise and fall, and bloody deeds await all…

GATHERING OF MIGHT

This is a Gathering of Might battle for two or more players. Use the Gathering of Might rules from pages 36-41.

THE ARMIES

Each side picks armies, as described on page 36.

SET-UP

Choose one of the three set-up methods, as described on page 37. Units must be set up wholly within their side's territory more than 9" from enemy territory.

GLORIOUS VICTORY

The side that has scored the most victory points (see below) at the end of the fifth battle round wins a **minor victory**, unless they win by 10 or more victory points in which case they win a **major victory**. If both sides have the same number of victory points, the result is a **draw**.

VICTORY POINTS

Each side gains a number of victory points at the end of each turn depending on the number of enemy units that were destroyed during that turn. Each side should keep a running total of the number of victory points they have scored as the game progresses. Victory points are scored as follows, and are cumulative:

- 1 victory point is scored for each enemy unit destroyed that turn.

- +1 victory point is scored if the combined Wounds characteristic of an enemy unit destroyed that turn is 20 or more; +2 if it is 30 or more, and so on.

- +1 victory point is scored for each enemy **Monster** destroyed that turn.

- +1 victory point is scored for each enemy **Hero** destroyed that turn.

- +3 victory points are scored if the enemy warlord's general was destroyed that turn.

For example, at the end of a side's turn the following enemy units have been destroyed:

- *1 unit of 3 Mighty Skullcrushers – 1 victory point.*

- *1 unit of 20 Bloodreavers – 1 victory point, +1 victory point for destroying a unit with a combined Wounds characteristic of 20.*

- *1 Khorgorath – 1 victory point, +1 victory point for destroying a Monster.*

- *1 Bloodthirster of Insensate Rage (the warlord's general) – 1 victory point, +1 victory point for destroying a Monster, +1 victory point for destroying a Hero, +3 victory points for destroying the warlord's general.*

The side scores a total of 11 victory points for this turn.

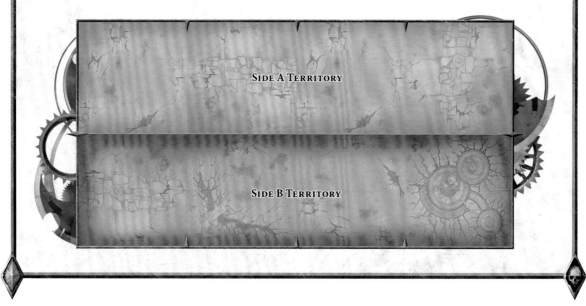

SIDE A TERRITORY

SIDE B TERRITORY

MATCHED
PLAY GAMES

People play Warhammer Age of Sigmar for all kinds of reasons. Many want to play games that test their skill as the commander of an army, in as evenly balanced a competition as possible. If the thought of games like this appeals to you, then read through the matched play rules detailed on the following pages to learn more.

There are countless benefits to matched play games. While narrative play games allow you to assemble your army based on a theme or story, and open play games enable you to include any models you like, matched play games give you the option to fight battles with forces that are intentionally balanced against one another.

A battle between armies that are equally balanced makes for a decisive test of your skill as a player, and the outcome of such a clash will always be hard to predict. Once you have settled on an army to use, you essentially have a pick-up-and-play force that you can bring to any table, against any opponent, and there's no need to agree on the setting and story of a battle as you would in an open or narrative play game. Matched play is ideal for tournaments and school leagues, as it provides clear guidelines on the size and strength of the armies taking part, as well as ensuring that all battles are as fair as they can be. Also, putting limits on both sides makes it easier to control how long a game will last, and as such, matched play is perfect for a quick battle in your local club or games store.

The following section offers more details on playing matched play games, providing inspiring methods for building and expanding your army. You will also find up-to-date Pitched Battle profiles to help you calculate the points cost of your army when using these rules. But however fascinating and enjoyable it is to design a perfect army, a true general will only be satisfied after their force has sallied forth and proven its worth on the battlefield. Matched play beckons – and glory awaits you!

INTRODUCING MATCHED PLAY

In the Mortal Realms, armies come in all shapes and sizes, each with its unique strengths and weaknesses. To truly test a general's mettle as a commander, there needs to be a level playing field that accounts for the variety of forces abroad in the Age of Sigmar. This is the goal of matched play.

The main differences between matched play and open play lie in army selection and battleplan design. Matched play games include rules that allow players to pick armies of equal power, and the battleplans written for matched play games are designed to provide tactically challenging games where each side has a more-or-less equal chance of winning.

The emphasis of matched play gaming is on planning, tactics and military nous, so it is the perfect format for those who consider themselves accomplished strategists and savvy commanders. While narrative and open play games can vary greatly in scope and content, presenting you with all manner of scenarios to battle through, matched play games are all about you and your army, the models you select and the tactics you use. They are driven by every player's desire for a satisfying and well-earned victory.

MATCHED PLAY ARMIES

As you will see, there are a number of ways to choose an army for a matched play game. Later in this section you will find our Pitched Battle rules, which can be used to pit your matched play army against those of fellow players. It uses a comprehensive points-based system that assigns a value to every unit available in the Warhammer Age of Sigmar range. Using this system, you and your opponent can assemble your armies based on a prearranged total of points so as to ensure that your forces are as equally matched as possible. Also included in this section are twelve battleplans, which have been designed to work with the Pitched Battle rules to provide players with different sets of tactical challenges to overcome.

There are other methods of choosing an army that don't involve adding up points, but still suit the matched play format. For example, you could use the Wounds characteristics listed on each unit's warscroll as a guideline, either setting an upper limit for the number of wounds a unit can have, or a fixed total of wounds that an army can have as a whole.

Whichever method you use, assembling an army for a matched play game is an important part of the process, and an interesting challenge in its own right. Do you spend a lot of points on one high-powered model and risk being overrun by a larger force? Do you allocate your points evenly on a versatile middleweight force? Your knowledge of the units available to you will be pivotal in this selection process, and knowledge of your opponent's force can be just as vital. These choices may be hard to make at first, but once you've found the perfect balance, you'll be able to use the same formula again and again to great effect, and this in turn can guide you when it comes to expanding your collection.

MATCHED PLAY BATTLEPLANS

In order to create a fair and balanced contest, matched play games have a method of setting up terrain, deploying armies, and determining the winner that is as even as possible for both sides.

Because of the desire to create an even contest, the battleplans for matched play tend to be quite simple, and both armies will usually be set up in a territory near one table edge.

Victory conditions can be more complex, but will almost always be the same for both sides (a process called 'mirroring'). Some common victory conditions in matched play battleplans include determining which side has slain the most enemy units after a certain number of battle rounds, and assigning victory points to players who are able to take control of objectives set up at the start of the game.

The Pitched Battle battleplans you'll find later on in this section use a combination of these two methods, with players winning points for destroying the enemy and capturing objectives to determine the winner.

However, whatever rules are actually used, the aim is always to create as even a contest as possible between the two armies, and this usually leads to fairly straightforward 'line up and fight' battles with mirrored victory conditions for both sides. The overall effect of this is a format that is ideal for 'pick-up' games between two players that have not met each other before. Matched play battleplans allow a player to simply go ahead and collect an army, choosing whichever models they like within the constraints of the army list, and then turn up at a club or gaming event, find an opponent, and play – knowing that the game will be as fair and even as possible.

GAMING CLUBS

A wonderful feature of the Games Workshop hobby is the degree to which it enables collectors to socialise. Hobbyists can connect via organised clubs, meet up, make friends, and play games of Warhammer Age of Sigmar in a friendly and supportive environment. The Internet makes this process easier than ever,

especially for those who can't easily get to a Games Workshop store.

A good start would be to search the Internet for 'Warhammer clubs' and the name of your town. You'll see which are popular, and chances are there's one close to you.

TOURNAMENTS

Throughout the wargaming hobby world, gaming events and tournaments take place virtually every weekend. Wherever you are, you're likely to find a tournament you can reach in the near future, and they're well worth attending.

Not only will you get to meet up with a warm and welcoming community of fellow hobbyists, but you'll get to play some great games, and see some truly amazing-looking armies. Often, special 'house' rules will have been created for the event, and no two tournaments are ever the same, keeping things exciting and interesting.

To find one near you, simply type 'Age of Sigmar tournament' and your town or area into an Internet search engine and get ready to go to war.

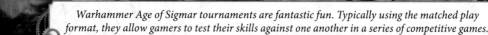

Warhammer Age of Sigmar tournaments are fantastic fun. Typically using the matched play format, they allow gamers to test their skills against one another in a series of competitive games.

PITCHED BATTLES

The following rules allow you to play a Pitched Battle, either as a one-off game, or as part of a tournament. These rules are designed to allow players to take part with the minimum of fuss, making them ideal for matched play pick-up games at clubs or gaming events.

To play a Pitched Battle, you and your opponent will first need to decide what type of Pitched Battle game you want to fight, and then pick your armies. The type of game you pick will determine how big the battle will be – the larger the battle, the more points you will have to spend on units for your army, but the longer the game will take.

There are three different types of Pitched Battle to choose from:

Game Type	Game Length
Vanguard	Up to 1 ½ hours
Battlehost	2 to 2 ½ hours
Warhost	3 or more hours

After you have agreed what type of game you want to play, look it up on the chart above. The chart lists the number of points each player has to spend on the units for their army, and what limitations apply to the types of unit you can bring. Each player must pick the units they will use for their army as described next.

PICKING YOUR ARMY

Each unit in a Pitched Battle is assigned a points value and a minimum and maximum unit size in its Pitched Battle profile. Pitched Battle profiles can be found on pages 63-87 of this book, or in the book where the warscroll for the unit appears. The game type you have chosen for your battle determines how many points you can spend on the units in your army. The combined points of the units in your army must not exceed the number of points shown on the chart. For example, in a Battlehost game, you can each field up to 2,000 points worth of units.

In a Pitched Battle game you must pick an allegiance for your army as described in the core rules. All of the units in the army must either have that allegiance, or be allied to that allegiance (see Allied Units, below).

PITCHED BATTLE CHART	Vanguard	Battlehost	Warhost
Points	1,000	2,000	2,500
Leaders	1-4	1-6	1-8
Battleline	2+	3+	4+
Artillery	0-2	0-4	0-5
Behemoths	0-2	0-4	0-5
Other Units	Any number	Any number	Any number
Allied Units (pts)	≤ 200	≤ 400	≤ 500

Endless spells have Pitched Battle profiles and a points cost. By paying the spell's points cost, all **Wizards** in the player's army know that endless spell, and the player can use (and re-use) one endless spell model of the appropriate type in the battle. A player cannot take the same endless spell model more than once for their army, but can take any number of different endless spell models (for example, you could not take two Balewind Vortex models).

BATTLEFIELD ROLES

Some units are assigned a battlefield role in their Pitched Battle profile. A unit's battlefield role is based on how it is used in a battle.

The Pitched Battle chart above lists the minimum number of Leaders and Battleline units you must include in a Pitched Battle army, and the maximum number of Leaders, Artillery, and Behemoth units it can include. A model that is a Leader and a Behemoth counts as one Leader and one Behemoth in your army.

ALLIED UNITS

In a Pitched Battle, the number of points that can be spent on allies from the player's total points allowance is shown on the Pitched Battle chart above. For example, a player playing a Battlehost game can spend up to 400 of their 2,000 points on allied units. This is in addition to the restrictions that normally apply to taking allied units.

Allied units are not included when working out the number of Battleline units in the army. They do count towards the maximum number of Leader, Behemoth and Artillery units that can be included in the army.

WARSCROLL BATTALIONS

If a player's army includes the units needed to field a warscroll battalion, then the player can include the battalion as part of their army by paying the points cost for it as shown on its Pitched Battle profile. You must pay the cost of the units in the battalion normally – the points value listed for each battalion is an extra cost that allows you to use it.

PITCHED BATTLE VARIATIONS

If both players agree, you can use either or both of the following variations to the way that the armies are picked:

You can agree to modify the points allowed for a Pitched Battle by plus or minus 250 points. For example, you might agree to play a 750 point Vanguard game, or a 2,750 point Warhost game.

You can agree to use points on their own. When playing a points-only game, ignore the limits on the number of Leader, Battleline, Behemoth and Artillery units you can take – you can take any units you like as long as they do not exceed the points limit you have set for your game.

ARMY ROSTER

Once you have picked your army, record the details on a piece of paper (your army roster), and show it to your opponent before setting up your army at the start of the battle.

The roster must include a list of the units, warscroll battalions and endless spells included in your army, what size the units are, details of weapons and equipment they have, the army's allegiance, which units are allies, the number of command points you have, and which model is the army's general. In a Pitched Battle, your general must be a Leader, and may not be an ally.

If your general is slain in a Pitched Battle game, do not select a new one.

If your army includes any units that are given keywords when they are set up, such as units with a Mark of Chaos, then these must be written down when the unit is added to the roster.

You must also record the allegiance abilities you have chosen for your army, the spells that are known by the wizards in your army, any artefacts or other items wielded by heroes in your army, and what command trait you have chosen for your general.

TRIUMPHS & COMMAND POINTS

Do not roll on the Triumph table in the core rules if you won your last battle. Instead, if one player has more points left over than their opponent after selecting their army, then they can roll on the Triumph table after both armies have been set up.

In a Pitched Battle, an army receives 1 extra command point for every 50 points that were not spent on units

for the army. For example, if you are fighting a Battlehost game and spend 1,895 points on units, then you will receive an extra 2 command points.

BATTLEPLANS

We have provided eighteen battleplans designed for use in Pitched Battles. Each offers a unique set of tactical challenges, and will provide each player with a chance to show their skill. To pick a battleplan, first roll a D3 to determine which of the three tables below you will use. Then roll a dice and consult the relevant table. The battleplans on table 1 are located in the *Warhammer Age of Sigmar Core Book*.

D6 Battleplan Table 1
1   Blood and Glory
2   Escalation
3   Border War
4   Three Places of Power
5   Gifts from the Heavens
6   Take and Hold

D6 Battleplan Table 2
1   Knife to the Heart (pg 50)
2   Total Conquest (pg 51)
3   Duality of Death (pg 52)
4   Battle for the Pass (pg 53)
5   Starstrike (pg 54)
6   Scorched Earth (pg 55)

D6 Battleplan Table 3
1   Total Commitment (pg 56)
2   Focal Points (pg 57)
3   The Better Part of Valour (pg 58)
4   Shifting Objectives (pg 59)
5   Places of Arcane Power (pg 60)
6   The Relocation Orb (pg 61)

BATTLEPLAN
KNIFE TO THE HEART

Two warlords are each struggling to gain control of a vital objective that lies deep in their opponent's territory. Both must strive to capture their objective first, ruthlessly wiping out any enemy incursions into their own territory while pushing their own forces deep into the enemy's heartland.

PITCHED BATTLE

Use the Pitched Battle rules from pages 48-49.

SET-UP

The players roll off, and the winner decides which territory each side will use. The territories are shown on the map below.

The players then alternate setting up units one at a time, starting with the player that won the roll-off. Units must be set up wholly within their own territory, more than 9" from enemy territory.

Continue to set up units until both players have set up their armies. If one player finishes first, the opposing player sets up the rest of the units in their army, one after another.

OBJECTIVES

This battle is fought to control two objectives. One objective is located in each territory 20" from the corner of the battlefield, as shown on the map below.

GLORIOUS VICTORY

Starting from the third battle round, one player immediately wins a **major victory** if they have control of both objectives.

If neither player has won by the end of the fifth battle round, or the amount of time allocated for the battle runs out, then each player adds up the points value of any enemy units that have been destroyed during the battle (excluding any new units that were added to the armies after the battle started). If one player has a higher total, they win a **minor victory**.

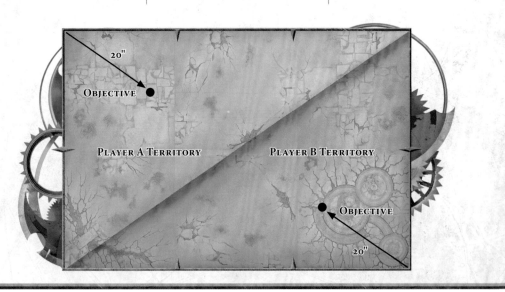

20"

OBJECTIVE

PLAYER A TERRITORY   PLAYER B TERRITORY

OBJECTIVE

20"

BATTLEPLAN
TOTAL CONQUEST

A blood-soaked battlefield is located at a vitally strategic location. Two armies stand upon this field of death, determined to drive their enemies from it and achieve total domination.

PITCHED BATTLE

Use the Pitched Battle rules from pages 48-49.

SET-UP

The players roll off, and the winner decides which territory each side will use. The territories are shown on the map below.

The players then alternate setting up units one at a time, starting with the player that won the roll-off. Units must be set up wholly within their own territory.

Continue to set up units until both players have set up their armies. If one player finishes first, the opposing player sets up the rest of the units in their army, one after another.

OBJECTIVES

This battle is fought to control four objectives. The objectives are located at the centre of each quarter of the battlefield, as shown on the map.

GLORIOUS VICTORY

The player with the most victory points at the end of the fifth battle round (or when the amount of time allocated for the battle runs out), wins a **major victory**.

If the players are tied on victory points at the end of the game, then each player adds up the points value of any enemy units that have been destroyed during the battle (excluding any new units that were added to the armies after the battle started). If one player has a higher total, they win a **minor victory**.

VICTORY POINTS

Each player scores victory points at the end of each of their turns for each objective they control, as follows:

For each objective the player controls, they score 1 victory point.

For each objective the player gained control of that turn that was previously controlled by their opponent, they score 1 additional victory point.

PLAYER A TERRITORY

OBJECTIVE

OBJECTIVE

3"

33"

15"

9"

9"

OBJECTIVE

OBJECTIVE

27"

PLAYER B TERRITORY

15"

BATTLEPLAN
DUALITY OF DEATH

Two focal points of incredible power lie close to each other. Either place will grant a hero or monstrous beast that stands upon it incredible power and everlasting life – but only if they can defeat the jealous enemies that wish to steal the location for themselves!

PITCHED BATTLE

Use the Pitched Battle rules from pages 48-49.

SET-UP

The players roll off, and the winner decides which territory each side will use. The territories are shown on the map below.

The players then alternate setting up units one at a time, starting with the player that won the roll-off. Units must be set up wholly within their own territory.

Continue to set up units until both players have set up their armies. If one player finishes first, the opposing player sets up the rest of the units in their army, one after another.

OBJECTIVES

This battle is fought to control two objectives. Each is located on the centre line, one in the middle of the left-hand half of the battlefield, and the other in the middle of the right-hand half of the battlefield, as shown on the map.

The normal rules for controlling an objective are not used in this battle. Instead, a player controls an objective if a **HERO** or Behemoth from their army is within 3" of the objective at the end of any type of move apart from a retreat move. The player loses control of the objective if the **HERO** or Behemoth finishes a subsequent move more than 3" from the objective.

Only one **HERO** or Behemoth can control each objective at a time – if more than one is eligible, then the first to arrive controls it. If a **HERO** or Behemoth slays an enemy **HERO** or Behemoth controlling an objective, then they immediately gain control of it if they are within 3" of it.

GLORIOUS VICTORY

The player with the most victory points at the end of the fifth battle round (or when the amount of time allocated for the battle runs out) wins a **major victory**.

If the players are tied on victory points at the end of the game, then each player adds up the points value of any enemy units that have been destroyed during the battle (excluding any new units that were added to the armies after the battle started). If one player has a higher total, they win a **minor victory**.

VICTORY POINTS

Each player scores victory points at the end of each of their turns for each objective they control. The number of victory points is equal to the number of consecutive turns the player has controlled the objective for; 1 on the turn they gained control, 2 at the end of the second turn, and so on.

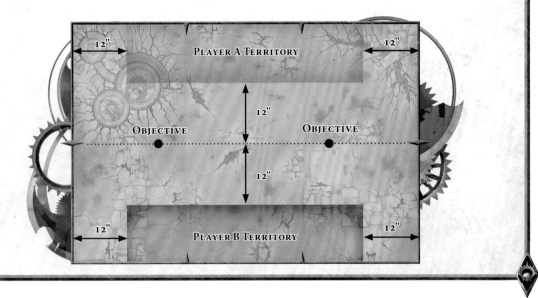

BATTLEPLAN
BATTLE FOR THE PASS

Many kingdoms in the Mortal Realms are separated by towering mountain ranges that can only be navigated by traversing a narrow pass. These defiles are of vital strategic importance, and many blood battles are fought over their control.

PITCHED BATTLE

Use the Pitched Battle rules from pages 48-49.

SET-UP

The players roll off, and the winner decides which territory each side will use. The territories are shown on the map below.

The players then alternate setting up units one at a time, starting with the player that won the roll-off. Units must be set up wholly within their own territory, more than 12" from enemy territory.

Continue to set up units until both players have set up their armies. If one player finishes first, the opposing player sets up the rest of the units in their army, one after another.

OBJECTIVES

This battle is fought to control four objectives. Two are located at the centre of each player's territory. The other two are located on the border between the players' territories, as shown on the map.

GLORIOUS VICTORY

The player with the most victory points at the end of the fifth battle round (or when the amount of time allocated for the battle runs out) wins a **major victory**.

If the players are tied on victory points at the end of the game, then each player adds up the points value of any enemy units that have been destroyed during the battle (excluding any new units that were added to the armies after the battle started). If one player has a higher total, they win a **minor victory**.

VICTORY POINTS

Each player scores victory points at the end of each of their turns for each objective they control, as follows:

If a player controls the objective in their own territory, they score 1 victory point.

For each objective the player controls on the border between the territories, they score 2 victory points.

If a player controls the objective in their opponent's territory, they score 4 victory points.

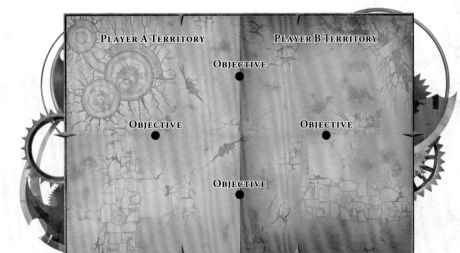

PLAYER A TERRITORY   PLAYER B TERRITORY

OBJECTIVE

OBJECTIVE   OBJECTIVE

OBJECTIVE

BATTLEPLAN
STARSTRIKE

In certain places in the Mortal Realms, the land is bombarded by fragments of magical ore that fall burning from the skies. These remnants of stars are coveted by ambitious warlords, as they can be used to forge deadly blades that will cut through any armour.

PITCHED BATTLE

Use the Pitched Battle rules from pages 48-49.

SET-UP

The players roll off, and the winner decides which territory each side will use. The territories are shown on the map below.

The players then alternate setting up units one at a time, starting with the player that won the roll-off. Units must be set up wholly within their own territory, more than 12" from enemy territory.

Continue to set up units until both players have set up their armies. If one player finishes first, the opposing player sets up the rest of the units in their army, one after another.

OBJECTIVES

This battle is fought to control three objectives, which are set up during the battle.

One is set up on the border between the two player's territories in the second battle round, and two more are set up in the third round, one in each player's territory. Set up the objectives at the start of the battle round, before the roll to determine who has the first turn is made. Roll a dice and refer to the map below to determine where each objective is set up.

GLORIOUS VICTORY

The player with the most victory points at the end of the fifth battle round (or when the amount of time allocated for the battle runs out) wins a **major victory**.

If the players are tied on victory points at the end of the game, then each player adds up the points value of any enemy units that have been destroyed during the battle (excluding any new units that were added to the armies after the battle started). If one player has a higher total, they win a **minor victory**.

VICTORY POINTS

Each player scores victory points at the end of each of their turns for each objective they control. The number of victory points is equal to the number of the current battle round. For example, a player that controls 1 objective at the end of their turn in the third battle round scores 3 victory points.

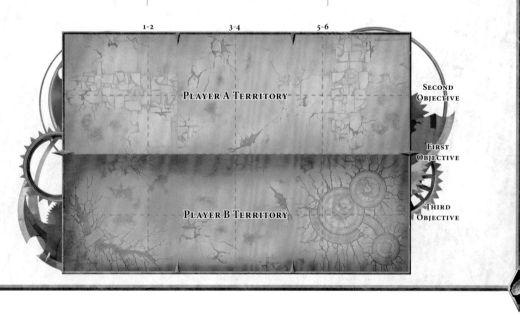

PLAYER A TERRITORY

PLAYER B TERRITORY

SECOND OBJECTIVE

FIRST OBJECTIVE

THIRD OBJECTIVE

1-2   3-4   5-6

BATTLEPLAN
SCORCHED EARTH

Sometimes battles are fought not to destroy the enemy, but to seize their resources and carry them off. Raiding parties will strike into enemy territory, capturing an objective and searching for any hidden treasures, before razing what remains to the ground to deny its use to the enemy.

PITCHED BATTLE

Use the Pitched Battle rules from pages 48-49.

SET-UP

The players roll off, and the winner decides which territory each side will use. The territories are shown on the map below.

The players then alternate setting up units one at a time, starting with the player that won the roll-off. Units must be set up wholly within their own territory, more than 9" from enemy territory.

Continue to set up units until both players have set up their armies. If one player finishes first, the opposing player sets up the rest of the units in their army, one after another.

OBJECTIVES

This battle is fought to control or raze six objectives. Three objectives are located in each player's territory, as shown on the map.

GLORIOUS VICTORY

The player with the most victory points at the end of the fifth battle round (or when the amount of time allocated for the battle runs out) wins a **major victory**.

If the players are tied on victory points at the end of the game, then each player adds up the points value of any enemy units that have been destroyed during the battle (excluding any new units that were added to the armies after the battle started). If one player has a higher total, they win a **minor victory**.

VICTORY POINTS

Each player scores 1 victory point at the end of each of their turns for each objective they control.

Starting from the second battle round, a player can raze an objective they control in enemy territory, scoring D3 victory points instead of 1 but removing the objective from play.

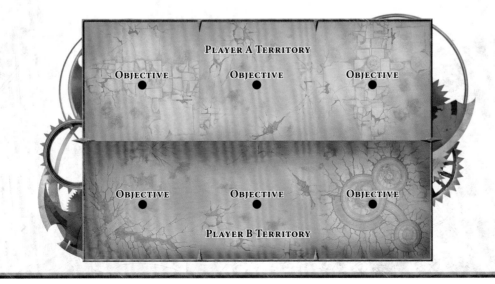

BATTLEPLAN
TOTAL COMMITMENT

A battle has been raging for days between two equally matched opponents. Both armies are committed to the fight, and neither side has any reserves left to draw upon.

PITCHED BATTLE

Use the Pitched Battle rules from pages 48-49.

SET-UP

The players roll off, and the winner decides which territory each side will use. The territories are shown on the map below.

The players then alternate setting up units one at a time, starting with the player that won the roll-off. Units must be set up wholly within their own territory, more than 9" from enemy territory.

Continue to set up units until both players have set up their armies. If one player finishes first, the opposing player sets up the rest of the units in their army, one after another.

NO RESERVES

In this battle, all units must be set up on the battlefield before the battle begins. Any unit that is set up as a reserve is destroyed and all of the models in the unit are slain.

OBJECTIVES

This battle is fought to control four objectives. Two objectives are located in each player's territory, as shown on the map.

GLORIOUS VICTORY

The player with the most victory points at the end of the fifth battle round (or when the amount of time allocated for the battle runs out) wins a **major victory**.

If the players are tied on victory points at the end of the game, then each player adds up the points value of any enemy units that have been destroyed during the battle (excluding any new units that were added to the armies after the battle started). If one player has a higher total, they win a **minor victory**.

VICTORY POINTS

Each player scores victory points at the end of each of their turns for each objective they control, as follows:

For each objective the player controls in their own territory, they score 1 victory point.

For each objective the player controls in their opponent's territory, they score 3 victory points.

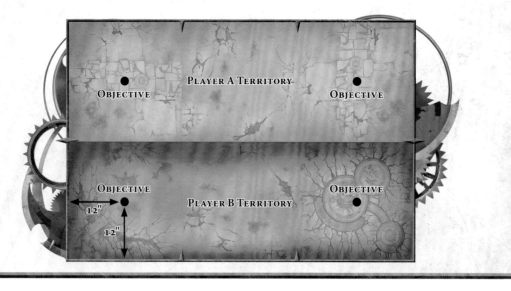

OBJECTIVE **PLAYER A TERRITORY** OBJECTIVE

OBJECTIVE **PLAYER B TERRITORY** OBJECTIVE

12"

12"

BATTLEPLAN
FOCAL POINTS

In this region, five focal points of geomantic energy are arranged in a square formation. Energy surges between these focal points, and it can be harnessed for use in rituals of awesome power.

PITCHED BATTLE
Use the Pitched Battle rules from pages 48-49.

SET-UP
The players roll off, and the winner decides which territory each side will use. The territories are shown on the map below.

The players then alternate setting up units one at a time, starting with the player that won the roll-off. Units must be set up wholly within their own territory, more than 9" from enemy territory.

Continue to set up units until both players have set up their armies. If one player finishes first, the opposing player sets up the rest of the units in their army, one after another.

OBJECTIVES
This battle is fought to control five objectives. One is located at the centre of the battlefield and two in each player's territory, as shown on the map.

GLORIOUS VICTORY
The player with the most victory points at the end of the fifth battle round (or when the amount of time allocated for the battle runs out) wins a **major victory**.

If the players are tied on victory points at the end of the game, then each player adds up the points value of any enemy units that have been destroyed during the battle (excluding any new units that were added to the armies after the battle started). If one player has a higher total, they win a **minor victory**.

VICTORY POINTS
Each player scores victory points for the objectives they control at the end of each of their turns, as follows:

If a player controls objectives one and three, they score 3 victory points.

If a player controls objectives two and four, they score 3 victory points.

If a player controls the central objective, they score 2 victory points.

If a player controls any other objective, they score 1 victory point for each objective.

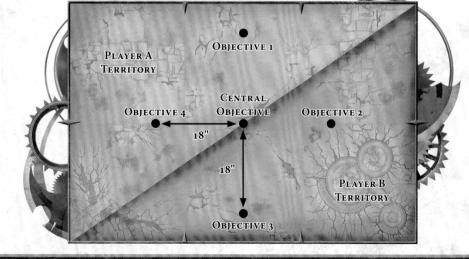

PLAYER A TERRITORY

OBJECTIVE 1

OBJECTIVE 4   CENTRAL OBJECTIVE   OBJECTIVE 2

18"

18"

PLAYER B TERRITORY

OBJECTIVE 3

BATTLEPLAN
THE BETTER PART OF VALOUR

It is important to learn when to hold on in order to ensure victory, and when to fall back in the face of unbeatable odds. A battle can be decided by the general most capable of resolving this difficult dilemma.

PITCHED BATTLE

Use the Pitched Battle rules from pages 48-49.

SET-UP

The players roll off, and the winner decides which territory each side will use. The territories are shown on the map below.

The players then alternate setting up units one at a time, starting with the player that won the roll-off. Units must be set up wholly within their own territory, more than 9" from enemy territory.

Continue to set up units until both players have set up their armies. If one player finishes first, the opposing player sets up the rest of the units in their army, one after another.

OBJECTIVES

This battle is fought to control six objectives. Three are located in each player's territory, as shown on the map.

GLORIOUS VICTORY

The player with the most victory points at the end of the fifth battle round (or when the amount of time allocated for the battle runs out) wins a **major victory**.

If the players are tied on victory points at the end of the game, then each player adds up the points value of any enemy units that have been destroyed during the battle (excluding any new units that were added to the armies after the battle started). If one player has a higher total, they win a **minor victory**.

VICTORY POINTS

At the end of each of their turns, a player can choose to destroy one or more of the objectives they control in order to score the following victory points:

If the player gained control of the objective in this turn, they score 1 victory point.

If the player controlled the objective at the end of their last turn, and has not lost control of it since, they score 2 victory points.

If the player controlled the objective at the end of their turn before last, and has not lost control of it since, they score 4 victory points.

If the player gained control of the objective in the first battle round, and has not lost control of it by the end of their turn in the fifth battle round, they score 8 victory points.

If more than one of these criteria applies, use the one that scores the most victory points. Once destroyed, an objective is removed from play.

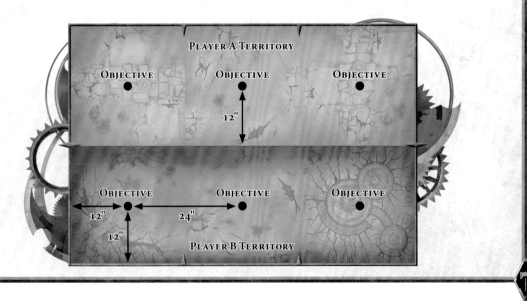

BATTLEPLAN
SHIFTING OBJECTIVES

In order to be successful, a general must learn to react with lightning swiftness to the changing conditions of battle, striking with all their might first in one direction and then in another in order to ensure victory.

PITCHED BATTLE

Use the Pitched Battle rules from pages 48-49.

SET-UP

The players roll off, and the winner decides which territory each side will use. The territories are shown on the map below.

The players then alternate setting up units one at a time, starting with the player that won the roll-off. Units must be set up wholly within their own territory.

Continue to set up units until both players have set up their armies. If one player finishes first, the opposing player sets up the rest of the units in their army, one after another.

OBJECTIVES

This battle is fought to control three objectives. They are located in the area between each player's territory, as shown on the map.

PRIMARY AND SECONDARY OBJECTIVES

At the start of each battle round, before determining who has the first turn, roll a D3. The objective with the corresponding number is the primary objective for that battle round, and the other two objectives are the secondary objectives for that battle round.

GLORIOUS VICTORY

The player with the most victory points at the end of the fifth battle round (or when the amount of time allocated for the battle runs out) wins a **major victory**.

If the players are tied on victory points at the end of the game, then each player adds up the points value of any enemy units that have been destroyed during the battle (excluding any new units that were added to the armies after the battle started). If one player has a higher total, they win a **minor victory**.

VICTORY POINTS

Each player scores victory points for each objective they control at the end of each of their turns, as follows:

If the player controls the primary objective, they score 3 victory points.

For each secondary objective the player controls, they score 1 victory point.

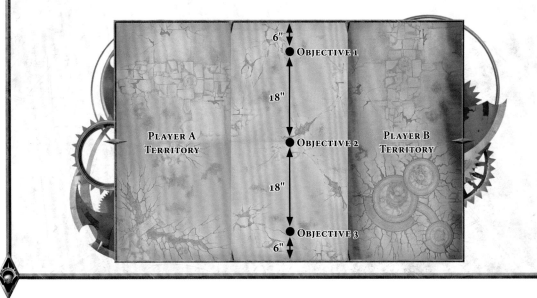

BATTLEPLAN
PLACES OF ARCANE POWER

The leaders of two rival armies have learned the location of three places of arcane power. If a warrior carrying a magical artefact or a wizard stands upon such a location, they can leech some of the arcane energy.

PITCHED BATTLE
Use the Pitched Battle rules from pages 48-49.

SET-UP
The players roll off, and the winner decides which territory each side will use. The territories are shown on the map below.

The players then alternate setting up units one at a time, starting with the player that won the roll-off. Units must be set up wholly within their own territory, more than 12" from enemy territory.

Continue to set up units until both players have set up their armies. If one player finishes first, the opposing player sets up the rest of the units in their army, one after another.

OBJECTIVES
This battle is fought to control three objectives. The objectives are located on the border between the players' territories, one in the middle of the battlefield and the others 18" from each corner, as shown on the map.

The normal rules for controlling an objective are not used in this battle. Instead, a player controls an objective if a friendly **Hero** with an artefact of power, or a friendly **Wizard**, is within 3" of the objective at the end of any type of move apart from a retreat move. The player loses control of the objective if the **Hero** or **Wizard** finishes a subsequent move more than 3" from the objective.

Only one model can control each objective – if more than one model is eligible, then the first to arrive controls it. If a **Hero** with an artefact of power or a **Wizard** slays an enemy model that is controlling an objective, then they immediately gain control of the objective if they are within 3" of it.

GLORIOUS VICTORY
The player with the most victory points at the end of the fifth battle round (or when the amount of time allocated for the battle runs out) wins a **major victory**.

If the players are tied on victory points at the end of the game, then each player adds up the points value of any enemy units that have been destroyed during the battle (excluding any new units that were added to the armies after the battle started). If one player has a higher total, they win a **minor victory**.

VICTORY POINTS
Each player scores victory points at the end of each of their turns for each objective they control. The number of victory points is equal to the number of consecutive turns the player has controlled the objective for; 1 on the turn they gained control, 2 at the end of the second turn, and so on.

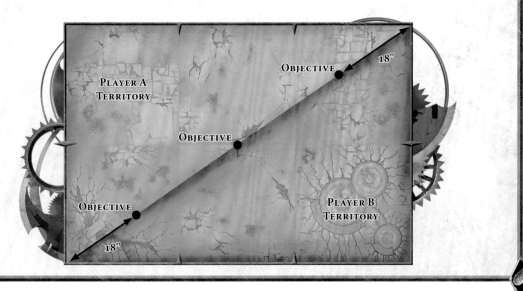

BATTLEPLAN
THE RELOCATION ORB

Relocation orbs are rare magical phenomena that can materialise anywhere in the Mortal Realms. They are highly prized for the potent energies they emit, which can be siphoned for use in numerous types of arcane ritual.

PITCHED BATTLE

Use the Pitched Battle rules from pages 48-49.

SET-UP

The players roll off, and the winner decides which territory each side will use. The territories are shown on the map below.

The players then alternate setting up units one at a time, starting with the player that won the roll-off. Units must be set up wholly within their own territory.

Continue to set up units until both players have set up their armies. If one player finishes first, the opposing player sets up the rest of the units in their army, one after another.

OBJECTIVES

This battle is fought to control one objective. It starts the battle located at the centre of the battlefield, and changes location at the end of each battle round as described below.

When determining control of an objective, each **HERO** with an artefact of power, and each **WIZARD**, that is within 3" of the objective counts as 20 models instead of only 1.

RELOCATING THE OBJECTIVE

The objective relocates to a new position on the battlefield at the end of each battle round. Control of the objective is lost when it relocates.

To determine the objective's new location, roll a dice. The objective relocates to the position indicated by the arrow on the map that corresponds to the dice roll.

If the relocation roll is 2-5, the objective remains at the new location until the end of the following battle round. If the relocation roll was a 1 or 6, then the objective relocates again immediately. Make a new relocation roll and move the objective to the position indicated by the new roll. It is possible for the objective to relocate several times in a row if the relocation roll is a 1 or a 6 each time.

GLORIOUS VICTORY

The player with the most victory points at the end of the fifth battle round (or when the amount of time allocated for the battle runs out) wins a **major victory**.

If the players are tied on victory points at the end of the game, then each player adds up the points value of any enemy units that have been destroyed during the battle (excluding any new units that were added to the armies after the battle started). If one player has a higher total, they win a **minor victory**.

VICTORY POINTS

Each player scores victory points if they control the objective at the end of each of their turns, as follows:

If the player controls the objective and had the first turn in the current battle round, they score 1 victory point.

If the player controls the objective and had the second turn in the current battle round, they score 3 victory points.

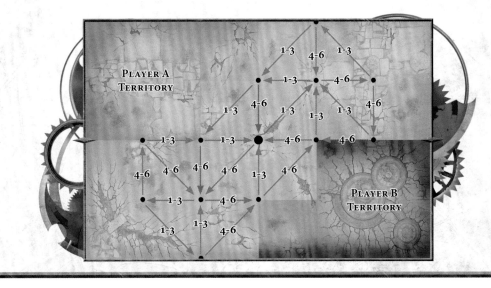

PITCHED BATTLE PROFILES

On the following pages you will find the Pitched Battle points values, unit sizes and battlefield roles for the units that can be used in Warhammer Age of Sigmar Pitched Battle games.

Pitched Battle profiles are organised by Grand Alliance and by book or faction. For example, the Pitched Battle profiles for Stormcast Eternal Liberators can be found in the Order Grand Alliance section, on the Stormcast Eternal table, while the profiles for Khorne Bloodbound units can be found in the Chaos Grand Alliance section, on the Blades of Khorne table. The profiles for scenery and endless spells appear on the table for their respective books.

Each unit you take in a Pitched Battle army costs the number of points indicated on its Pitched Battle profile. Spending the appropriate number of points on a unit allows you to take a minimum-sized unit of that sort, with any of the optional upgrades to which it is entitled and which you wish to take. Any Artillery unit that needs a crew receives the associated crew unit at no additional cost in points.

Larger units are taken in multiples of their minimum unit size, as long as the number of models in the unit does not exceed its maximum unit size. When you take a larger unit, multiply the cost of the unit by the same amount as you multiplied its minimum size. For example, a unit has a minimum unit size of 5 models, a maximum unit size of 20 models, and a points value of 100 points. It can be taken as a unit of 5, 10, 15 or 20 models, for a cost of 100, 200, 300 or 400 points.

UNDERSTRENGTH UNITS

Sometimes you may find that you do not have enough models to field a unit at full strength; if this is the case, you must still pay the full cost of the unit. For example, if you decided to field a unit of 3 Liberators, rather than a full-strength unit with 5 models, the unit would still cost 100 points.

MASSIVE REGIMENTS

Sometimes a unit will have two points values separated by a slash: '60/200' for example. When this is the case, the second points value is for a unit with the maximum number of models. Such units are referred to as massive regiments. For example, the points value listed for Gors is 80/210, and their maximum unit size is 30. If you take a massive regiment of 30 Gors, it will have a cost of 210 points rather than 240.

UNIQUE UNITS

Units that are listed as 'Unique' on their Pitched Battle profile can only be included once in a Pitched Battle army. Such units are named characters as described in the Allegiance Abilities section of the core rules.

ALLIES

At the end of each Grand Alliance section you will find an Allies table that lists the eligible allies for the factions that belong to that Grand Alliance. A unit that has any of the keywords listed on the Allies table on its warscroll can be taken as an allied unit by an army from that faction. For example, a Stormcast Eternals army can take any unit with the ORDER keyword as an allied unit.

UPDATED PROFILES JUNE 2018

Whenever we publish a new edition of the *General's Handbook* or a new battletome, we review, update and fine-tune the Pitched Battle profiles for all of the models. This means that the profiles printed here take precedence over any profiles with an earlier publication date, and also take precedence over profiles that have no publication date at all. Profiles that have changed since their last publication are marked on the following pages with this symbol: ✶

CHAOS PITCHED BATTLE PROFILES

BRAYHERDS UNIT	UNIT SIZE MIN	MAX	POINTS	BATTLEFIELD ROLE	NOTES
Gors	10	30	80/210	Battleline	
Ungors	10	40	60/200	Battleline	
✳ Beastlord	1	1	90	Leader	
✳ Great Bray-Shaman	1	1	100	Leader	
✳ Bestigors	10	30	120/300		Battleline in Brayherds army
Tuskgor Chariots	1	4	60		
✳ Ungor Raiders	10	40	80		Battleline in Brayherds army
✳ Wildstalker Brayherd	-	-	210	Warscroll Battalion	

BLADES OF KHORNE UNIT	UNIT SIZE MIN	MAX	POINTS	BATTLEFIELD ROLE	NOTES
✳ Skull Cannons	1	3	150	Artillery	
✳ Bloodletters	10	30	120/320	Battleline	
Bloodreavers	10	40	70/240	Battleline	
Blood Warriors	5	30	100/520	Battleline	
Aspiring Deathbringer	1	1	80	Leader	
Aspiring Deathbringer with Goreaxe and Skullhammer	1	1	100	Leader	
Bloodmaster, Herald of Khorne	1	1	80	Leader	
✳ Bloodsecrator	1	1	140	Leader	
Bloodstoker	1	1	80	Leader	
Blood Throne	1	1	120	Leader	
Exalted Deathbringer	1	1	80	Leader	
Exalted Deathbringer with Impaling Spear	1	1	80	Leader	
✳ Karanak	1	1	90	Leader	Unique
✳ Korghos Khul	1	1	180	Leader	Unique
Lord of Khorne on Juggernaut	1	1	140	Leader	
✳ Mighty Lord of Khorne	1	1	120	Leader	
Scyla Anfingrimm	1	1	100	Leader	Unique
Skarr Bloodwrath	1	1	80	Leader	Unique
Skullgrinder	1	1	80	Leader	
Skullmaster, Herald of Khorne	1	1	100	Leader	
Skulltaker	1	1	100	Leader	Unique
Slaughterpriest	1	1	100	Leader	
Slaughterpriest with Hackblade and Wrath-hammer	1	1	100	Leader	
Valkia the Bloody	1	1	140	Leader	Unique
Bloodthirster of Insensate Rage	1	1	260	Leader, Behemoth	
Bloodthirster of Unfettered Fury	1	1	260	Leader, Behemoth	
Skarbrand	1	1	400	Leader, Behemoth	Unique
✳ Wrath of Khorne Bloodthirster	1	1	320	Leader, Behemoth	
✳ Bloodcrushers	3	12	150		Battleline in Khorne army if general is a Skullmaster, Herald of Khorne
✳ Flesh Hounds	5	20	100		Battleline in Khorne army
✳ Khorgoraths	1	6	90		

BLADES OF KHORNE UNIT	UNIT SIZE MIN	MAX	POINTS	BATTLEFIELD ROLE	NOTES
Mighty Skullcrushers	3	12	140		Battleline in Khorne army if general is a Lord of Khorne on Juggernaut
✳ Skullreapers	5	20	170		
Wrathmongers	5	20	180		
Blood Host of Khorne	-	-	*220*	*Warscroll Battalion*	
✳ *Blood Hunt*	-	-	*180*	*Warscroll Battalion*	
Bloodbound Warband	-	-	*220*	*Warscroll Battalion*	
✳ *Bloodbound Warhorde*	-	-	*140*	*Warscroll Battalion*	
✳ *Bloodforged*	-	-	*160*	*Warscroll Battalion*	
✳ *The Bloodlords*	-	-	*100*	*Warscroll Battalion*	
Bloodthunder Stampede	-	-	*180*	*Warscroll Battalion*	
✳ *Brass Stampede*	-	-	*200*	*Warscroll Battalion*	
✳ *Charnel Host*	-	-	*200*	*Warscroll Battalion*	
✳ *Council of Blood*	-	-	*150*	*Warscroll Battalion*	
✳ *Daemon Legion of Khorne*	-	-	*140*	*Warscroll Battalion*	
Dark Feast	-	-	*200*	*Warscroll Battalion*	
✳ *Gore Pilgrims*	-	-	*200*	*Warscroll Battalion*	
✳ *The Gorechosen*	-	-	*160*	*Warscroll Battalion*	
✳ *Gorethunder Cohort*	-	-	*130*	*Warscroll Battalion*	
✳ *The Goretide*	-	-	*130*	*Warscroll Battalion*	
✳ *Murderhost*	-	-	*220*	*Warscroll Battalion*	
✳ *The Reapers of Vengeance*	-	-	*80*	*Warscroll Battalion*	
Red Headsmen	-	-	*160*	*Warscroll Battalion*	
✳ *The Skullfiend Tribe*	-	-	*70*	*Warscroll Battalion*	
✳ *Skullseeker Host*	-	-	*170*	*Warscroll Battalion*	
✳ *Skulltake*	-	-	*190*	*Warscroll Battalion*	
✳ *Slaughterborn*	-	-	*160*	*Warscroll Battalion*	

CHAOS GARGANTS UNIT	UNIT SIZE MIN	MAX	POINTS	BATTLEFIELD ROLE	NOTES
✳ Chaos Gargant	1	1	160	Behemoth	

CLANS ESHIN UNIT	UNIT SIZE MIN	MAX	POINTS	BATTLEFIELD ROLE	NOTES
Deathrunner	1	1	120	Leader	
Skaven Assassin	1	1	100	Leader	
✳ Verminlord Deceiver	1	1	300	Leader, Behemoth	
Gutter Runners	5	20	60/200		Battleline in Eshin army
Night Runners	10	40	100/360		Battleline in Eshin army

CLANS MOULDER UNIT	UNIT SIZE MIN	MAX	POINTS	BATTLEFIELD ROLE	NOTES
✳ Hell Pit Abomination	1	1	220	Behemoth	
✳ Packmaster	1	1	60	Leader	
Giant Rats	10	40	60/200		Battleline in Moulder army
✳ Rat Ogors	2	8	100		Battleline in Moulder army
✳ Rat Swarms	2	8	110		

CLANS PESTILENS UNIT	UNIT SIZE MIN	MAX	POINTS	BATTLEFIELD ROLE	NOTES
✷ Plagueclaw	1	1	160	Artillery	
Plague Priest with Plague Censer	1	1	80	Leader	
Plague Priest with Warpstone-tipped Staff	1	1	80	Leader	
✷ Plague Furnace	1	1	180	Leader, Behemoth	
Verminlord Corruptor	1	1	220	Leader, Behemoth	
Plague Censer Bearers	5	20	60		Battleline in Pestilens army
Plague Monks	10	40	70/240		Battleline in Pestilens army
✷ Congregation of Filth	-	-	170	Warscroll Battalion	
✷ Foulrain Congregation	-	-	190	Warscroll Battalion	
✷ Plaguesmog Congregation	-	-	140	Warscroll Battalion	
✷ Virulent Procession	-	-	160	Warscroll Battalion	

CLANS SKRYRE UNIT	UNIT SIZE MIN	MAX	POINTS	BATTLEFIELD ROLE	NOTES
Warp Lightning Cannon	1	1	180	Artillery	
Warplock Jezzails	3	12	140	Artillery	
✷ Doomwheel	1	1	120	Behemoth	
Arch-warlock	1	1	140	Leader	
Warlock Engineer	1	1	100	Leader	
Ratling Gun Weapon Team	1	1	80		
✷ Warp-grinder Weapon Team	1	1	80		
Warpfire Thrower Weapon Team	1	1	70		
Poisoned Wind Mortar Weapon Team	1	1	60		
Doom-flayer Weapon Team	1	1	60		
Skryre Acolytes	5	30	60/320		Battleline in Skryre army
✷ Stormfiends	3	9	290		Battleline in Skryre army
✷ Clan Skryre	-	-	80	Warscroll Battalion	Add the cost of each Enginecoven to the cost of the battalion
✷ Arkhspark Voltik	-	-	70	Enginecoven	
✷ Gascloud Chokelung	-	-	70	Enginecoven	
Gautfyre Skorch	-	-	150	Enginecoven	
✷ Rattlegauge Warplock	-	-	70	Enginecoven	
✷ Whyrlblade Threshik	-	-	70	Enginecoven	

CLANS VERMINUS UNIT	UNIT SIZE MIN	MAX	POINTS	BATTLEFIELD ROLE	NOTES
Clanrats	20	40	120/200	Battleline	
Skaven Warlord	1	1	100	Leader	
✷ Verminlord Warbringer	1	1	280	Leader, Behemoth	
✷ Stormvermin	10	30	140/500		Battleline in Verminus army

DAEMONS OF CHAOS UNIT	UNIT SIZE MIN	MAX	POINTS	BATTLEFIELD ROLE	NOTES
✷ Soul Grinder	1	1	260	Behemoth	
Be'lakor, Chaos Daemon Prince	1	1	280	Leader, Behemoth	Unique
Daemon Prince	1	1	160	Leader, Behemoth	
Furies	5	30	60/320		

DISCIPLES OF TZEENTCH UNIT	UNIT SIZE MIN	MAX	POINTS	BATTLEFIELD ROLE	NOTES
✳ Kairic Acolytes	10	40	80/300	Battleline	
✳ Pink Horrors of Tzeentch	10	30	200/540	Battleline	
✳ Tzaangors	10	30	180/480	Battleline	
✳ The Blue Scribes	1	1	140	Leader	Unique
✳ The Changeling	1	1	200	Leader	Unique
✳ Curseling, Eye of Tzeentch	1	1	160	Leader	
✳ Fatemaster	1	1	120	Leader	
✳ Gaunt Summoner & Chaos Familiars	1	1	180	Leader	
✳ Gaunt Summoner of Tzeentch	1	1	180	Leader	
✳ Herald of Tzeentch	1	1	140	Leader	
Herald of Tzeentch on Burning Chariot	1	1	200	Leader	
✳ Herald of Tzeentch on Disc	1	1	140	Leader	
✳ Magister	1	1	140	Leader	
✳ Ogroid Thaumaturge	1	1	180	Leader	
✳ Tzaangor Shaman	1	1	180	Leader	
✳ Kairos Fateweaver	1	1	380	Leader, Behemoth	Unique
✳ Lord of Change	1	1	380	Leader, Behemoth	
✳ Blue Horrors of Tzeentch	10	30	100		
✳ Brimstone Horrors of Tzeentch	10	30	70		
Burning Chariots of Tzeentch	1	3	160		Battleline in Tzeentch army if general is a Herald of Tzeentch on Burning Chariot
✳ Exalted Flamers of Tzeentch	1	6	100		
✳ Flamers of Tzeentch	3	12	160		
✳ Screamers of Tzeentch	3	12	100		
Tzaangor Enlightened	3	9	160		
✳ Tzaangor Skyfires	3	9	220		
✳ Aether-eater Host	-	-	130	Warscroll Battalion	
✳ Alter-kin Coven	-	-	130	Warscroll Battalion	
✳ Arcanite Cabal	-	-	180	Warscroll Battalion	
✳ Arcanite Cult	-	-	120	Warscroll Battalion	
✳ Changehost	-	-	180	Warscroll Battalion	
✳ Cult of the Transient Form	-	-	100	Warscroll Battalion	
✳ Multitudinous Host	-	-	240	Warscroll Battalion	
✳ Omniscient Oracles	-	-	130	Warscroll Battalion	
✳ Overseer's Fate-twisters	-	-	140	Warscroll Battalion	
Skyshoal Coven	-	-	130	Warscroll Battalion	
✳ The Eternal Conflagration	-	-	110	Warscroll Battalion	
✳ The Hosts Duplicitous	-	-	110	Warscroll Battalion	
✳ The Pyrofane Cult	-	-	140	Warscroll Battalion	
✳ Tzaangor Coven	-	-	110	Warscroll Battalion	
✳ Warpflame Host	-	-	100	Warscroll Battalion	
✳ Witchfyre Coven	-	-	120	Warscroll Battalion	

EVERCHOSEN UNIT	UNIT SIZE MIN	MAX	POINTS	BATTLEFIELD ROLE	NOTES
✳ Gaunt Summoner of Tzeentch	1	1	180	Leader	
✳ Archaon	1	1	660	Leader, Behemoth	Unique
✳ Varanguard	3	12	280		Battleline in Everchosen army

EVERCHOSEN UNIT	UNIT SIZE MIN	MAX	POINTS	BATTLEFIELD ROLE	NOTES
✴ Archaon's Grand Host	-	-	120	Warscroll Battalion	
✴ Bloodmarked Warband	-	-	160	Warscroll Battalion	
✴ Fatesworn Warband	-	-	160	Warscroll Battalion	
Overlords of Chaos	-	-	220	Warscroll Battalion	
✴ Plaguetouched Warband	-	-	160	Warscroll Battalion	
✴ Pleasurebound Warband	-	-	140	Warscroll Battalion	

HOSTS OF SLAANESH UNIT	UNIT SIZE MIN	MAX	POINTS	BATTLEFIELD ROLE	NOTES
Daemonettes of Slaanesh	10	30	100/270	Battleline	
Chaos Lord of Slaanesh	1	1	100	Leader	
Herald of Slaanesh	1	1	60	Leader	
Herald of Slaanesh on Exalted Seeker Chariot	1	1	160	Leader	
Herald of Slaanesh on Seeker Chariot	1	1	100	Leader	
Lord of Slaanesh on Daemonic Mount	1	1	140	Leader	
The Masque of Slaanesh	1	1	80	Leader	Unique
✴ Keeper of Secrets	1	1	260	Leader, Behemoth	
Exalted Seeker Chariots of Slaanesh	1	3	140		
Fiends of Slaanesh	3	9	140		
Hellflayers of Slaanesh	1	3	80		
Hellstriders of Slaanesh	5	20	100		
Seeker Chariots of Slaanesh	1	3	80		Battleline in Slaanesh army Battleline in Slaanesh army if general is a Herald of Slaanesh on Exalted Seeker Chariot
Seekers of Slaanesh	5	20	120		

MASTERCLAN UNIT	UNIT SIZE MIN	MAX	POINTS	BATTLEFIELD ROLE	NOTES
✴ Grey Seer	1	1	100	Leader	
✴ Lord Skreech Verminkin	1	1	300	Leader, Behemoth	Unique
Screaming Bell	1	1	200	Leader, Behemoth	
✴ Thanquol and Boneripper	1	1	400	Leader, Behemoth	Unique
Verminlord Warpseer	1	1	260	Leader, Behemoth	

MAGGOTKIN OF NURGLE UNIT	UNIT SIZE MIN	MAX	POINTS	BATTLEFIELD ROLE	NOTES
Plaguebearers	10	30	120/320	Battleline	
Epidemius, Tallyman of Nurgle	1	1	200	Leader	Unique
Festus the Leechlord	1	1	140	Leader	Unique
Gutrot Spume	1	1	140	Leader	Unique
Harbinger of Decay	1	1	160	Leader	
Horticulous Slimux	1	1	220	Leader	Unique
Lord of Afflictions	1	1	220	Leader	
Lord of Blights	1	1	140	Leader	
Lord of Plagues	1	1	140	Leader	
Poxbringer, Herald of Nurgle	1	1	120	Leader	
Sloppity Bilepiper, Herald of Nurgle	1	1	100	Leader	
Spoilpox Scrivener, Herald of Nurgle	1	1	100	Leader	
Sorcerer	1	1	120	Leader	
Bloab Rotspawned	1	1	260	Leader, Behemoth	Unique

MAGGOTKIN OF NURGLE UNIT	UNIT SIZE MIN	MAX	POINTS	BATTLEFIELD ROLE	NOTES
Great Unclean One	1	1	340	Leader, Behemoth	
Morbidex Twiceborn	1	1	260	Leader, Behemoth	Unique
Orghotts Daemonspew	1	1	260	Leader, Behemoth	Unique
Rotigus	1	1	340	Leader, Behemoth	Unique
The Glottkin	1	1	420	Leader, Behemoth	Unique
Beasts of Nurgle	1	6	100		
Nurglings	3	12	100		
Plague Drones	3	12	200		
Pusgoyle Blightlords	2	12	220		Battleline in Nurgle army if general is a Lord of Afflictions
Putrid Blightkings	5	20	160/580		Battleline in Nurgle army
Affliction Cyst	-	-	220	*Warscroll Battalion*	
Blight Cyst	-	-	220	*Warscroll Battalion*	
✳ *Plague Cyst*	-	-	200	*Warscroll Battalion*	
✳ *The Munificent Wanderers*	-	-	100	*Warscroll Battalion*	
Nurgle's Menagerie	-	-	240	*Warscroll Battalion*	
Tallyband of Nurgle	-	-	220	*Warscroll Battalion*	
✳ *Thricefold Befoulment*	-	-	120	*Warscroll Battalion*	
✳ *The Blessed Sons*	-	-	100	*Warscroll Battalion*	
Feculent Gnarlmaw	1	1	0	*Scenery*	

MONSTERS OF CHAOS UNIT	UNIT SIZE MIN	MAX	POINTS	BATTLEFIELD ROLE	NOTES
Chimera	1	1	220	Behemoth	
Cockatrice	1	1	100	Behemoth	
✳ Jabberslythe	1	1	140	Behemoth	
Mutalith Vortex Beast	1	1	200	Behemoth	
Slaughterbrute	1	1	180	Behemoth	
Centigors	5	20	80		
Chaos Warhounds	10	30	80/210		
✳ Harpies	5	20	60		
Razorgors	1	6	60		

SLAVES TO DARKNESS UNIT	UNIT SIZE MIN	MAX	POINTS	BATTLEFIELD ROLE	NOTES
✳ Chaos Marauders	20	40	120/200	Battleline	
Chaos Warriors	5	30	90/480	Battleline	
✳ Chaos Warshrine	1	1	160	Behemoth	
Chaos Lord on Daemonic Mount	1	1	140	Leader	
Chaos Sorcerer Lord	1	1	160	Leader	
Darkoath Chieftain	1	1	80	Leader	
Darkoath Warqueen	1	1	80	Leader	
Exalted Hero of Chaos	1	1	80	Leader	
✳ Lord of Chaos	1	1	140	Leader	
Slambo	1	1	80	Leader	Unique
Chaos Lord on Manticore	1	1	250	Leader, Behemoth	
Chaos Sorcerer Lord on Manticore	1	1	200	Leader, Behemoth	
Daemon Prince	1	1	160	Leader, Behemoth	
Chaos Chariots	1	3	80		Battleline in Slaves to Darkness army
Chaos Chosen	5	20	140		

SLAVES TO DARKNESS UNIT	UNIT SIZE MIN	MAX	POINTS	BATTLEFIELD ROLE	NOTES
Chaos Gorebeast Chariots	1	3	100		
Chaos Knights	5	20	160		Battleline in Slaves to Darkness army
Chaos Marauder Horsemen	5	30	90/480		Battleline in Slaves to Darkness army
Chaos Spawn	1	6	50		
✳ *Godsworn Champions of Ruin*	-	-	*170*	*Warscroll Battalion*	
✳ *Godswrath Warband*	-	-	*150*	*Warscroll Battalion*	
Ruinbringer Warband	-	-	*180*	*Warscroll Battalion*	

THUNDERSCORN UNIT	UNIT SIZE MIN	MAX	POINTS	BATTLEFIELD ROLE	NOTES
Dragon Ogor Shaggoth	1	1	160	Leader	
✳ Dragon Ogors	3	12	140		Battleline in Thunderscorn army

WARHERDS UNIT	UNIT SIZE MIN	MAX	POINTS	BATTLEFIELD ROLE	NOTES
✳ Cygor	1	1	180	Behemoth	
Ghorgon	1	1	200	Behemoth	
Doombull	1	1	120	Leader	
✳ Bullgors	3	12	160		Battleline in Warherds army

OTHER UNITS UNIT	UNIT SIZE MIN	MAX	POINTS	BATTLEFIELD ROLE	NOTES
Mutalith Vortex Beast of Tzeentch	1	1	200	Behemoth	
✳ Slaughterbrute of Khorne	1	1	170	Behemoth	

CHAOS	ALLIES
Brayherds	Chaos Gargants, Monsters of Chaos, Thunderscorn, Warherds
Clans Eshin	Clans Moulder, Clans Pestilens, Clans Skryre, Clans Verminus, Masterclan
Clans Moulder	Clans Eshin, Clans Pestilens, Clans Skryre, Clans Verminus, Masterclan
Clans Pestilens	Clans Eshin, Clans Moulder, Clans Skryre, Clans Verminus, Masterclan, Nurgle
Clans Skryre	Clans Eshin, Clans Moulder, Clans Pestilens, Clans Verminus, Masterclan
Clans Verminus	Clans Eshin, Clans Moulder, Clans Pestilens, Clans Skryre, Masterclan
Everchosen	Any CHAOS faction
Slaanesh	Brayherds, Chaos Gargants, Everchosen, Monsters of Chaos, Nurgle, Slaves to Darkness (excluding units with mark of KHORNE), Warherds
Khorne	Brayherds, Chaos Gargants, Everchosen, Monsters of Chaos, Nurgle, Slaves to Darkness (excluding units with mark of SLAANESH), Warherds
Nurgle	Brayherds, Chaos Gargants, Everchosen, Khorne, Monsters of Chaos, Slaanesh, Slaves to Darkness (excluding units with mark of TZEENTCH), Warherds
Slaves to Darkness	Brayherds, Chaos Gargants, Everchosen, Khorne, Nurgle, Slaanesh, Tzeentch, Warherds
Thunderscorn	Brayherds, Chaos Gargants, Monsters of Chaos, Warherds
Tzeentch	Chaos Gargants, Everchosen, Monsters of Chaos, Slaves to Darkness (excluding units with mark of NURGLE), Thunderscorn
Warherds	Brayherds, Chaos Gargants, Monsters of Chaos, Thunderscorn

DEATH PITCHED BATTLE PROFILES

FLESH-EATER COURTS UNIT	UNIT SIZE MIN	MAX	POINTS	BATTLEFIELD ROLE	NOTES
Crypt Ghouls	10	40	100/360	Battleline	
Terrorgheist	1	1	300	Behemoth	
Zombie Dragon	1	1	300	Behemoth	
✳ Abhorrant Ghoul King	1	1	140	Leader	
Crypt Ghast Courtier	1	1	80	Leader	
✳ Crypt Haunter Courtier	1	1	140	Leader	
Crypt Infernal Courtier	1	1	140	Leader	
Varghulf Courtier	1	1	160	Leader	
Abhorrant Ghoul King on Terrorgheist	1	1	400	Leader, Behemoth	
Abhorrant Ghoul King on Zombie Dragon	1	1	440	Leader, Behemoth	
Crypt Flayers	3	12	160		Battleline in Flesh-eater Courts army if general is a Crypt Infernal Courtier
Crypt Horrors	3	12	160		Battleline in Flesh-eater Courts army if general is a Crypt Haunter Courtier
✳ *Abattoir*	-	-	*130*	*Warscroll Battalion*	
✳ *Attendants at Court*	-	-	*160*	*Warscroll Battalion*	
✳ *Deadwatch*	-	-	*170*	*Warscroll Battalion*	
Flesh-eater Court	-	-	*120*	*Warscroll Battalion*	
✳ *Ghoul Patrol*	-	-	*180*	*Warscroll Battalion*	
✳ *King's Ghouls*	-	-	*130*	*Warscroll Battalion*	
✳ *Royal Family*	-	-	*150*	*Warscroll Battalion*	
✳ *Royal Menagerie*	-	-	*140*	*Warscroll Battalion*	
✳ *Royal Mordants*	-	-	*110*	*Warscroll Battalion*	

LEGIONS OF NAGASH UNIT	UNIT SIZE MIN	UNIT SIZE MAX	POINTS	BATTLEFIELD ROLE	NOTES
Dire Wolves	5	30	60/320	Battleline	
Skeleton Warriors	10	40	80/280	Battleline	
Zombies	10	60	60/320	Battleline	
Mortis Engine	1	1	180	Behemoth	
Terrorgheist	1	1	300	Behemoth	
Zombie Dragon	1	1	300	Behemoth	
Cairn Wraith	1	1	60	Leader	
Necromancer	1	1	110	Leader	
Tomb Banshee	1	1	80	Leader	
Vampire Lord	1	1	140	Leader	
Wight King with Baleful Tomb Blade	1	1	120	Leader	
Wight King with Black Axe	1	1	120	Leader	
Arkhan the Black, Mortarch of Sacrament	1	1	320	Leader, Behemoth	Unique
Bloodseeker Palanquin	1	1	320	Leader, Behemoth	
Coven Throne	1	1	260	Leader, Behemoth	
Mannfred, Mortarch of Night	1	1	420	Leader, Behemoth	Unique
Nagash, Supreme Lord of the Undead	1	1	800	Leader, Behemoth	Unique
Neferata, Mortarch of Blood	1	1	400	Leader, Behemoth	Unique
Prince Vhordrai	1	1	480	Leader, Behemoth	Unique
Vampire Lord on Zombie Dragon	1	1	440	Leader, Behemoth	
Bat Swarms	2	8	80		
Black Coach	1	1	120		
Black Knights	5	20	120		
✳ Blood Knights	5	15	240		Battleline in Soulblight army
Corpse Cart with Balefire Brazier	1	1	80		
Corpse Cart with Unholy Lodestone	1	1	80		
Fell Bats	3	12	80		
Grave Guard	5	30	80/420		Battleline in Grand Host of Nagash army
Hexwraiths	5	20	160		Battleline in Nighthaunt army
Morghast Archai	2	6	220		Battleline in Grand Host of Nagash army if general is Nagash
Morghast Harbingers	2	6	220		Battleline in Grand Host of Nagash army if general is Nagash
Spirit Hosts	3	12	120		Battleline in Nighthaunt army
Vargheists	3	12	160		
✳ Castellans of the Crimson Keep	-	-	150	Warscroll Battalion	
✳ Court of Nulahmia	-	-	110	Warscroll Battalion	
✳ Deathmarch	-	-	160	Warscroll Battalion	
✳ The First Cohort	-	-	160	Warscroll Battalion	
✳ Lords of Sacrament	-	-	130	Warscroll Battalion	
✳ Nightfall Pack	-	-	170	Warscroll Battalion	

NIGHTHAUNT UNIT	UNIT SIZE MIN	MAX	POINTS	BATTLEFIELD ROLE	NOTES
Chainrasp Horde	10	40	80/280	Battleline	
✳ Black Coach	1	1	280	Behemoth	
Cairn Wraith	1	1	60	Leader	
Dreadblade Harrow	1	1	100	Leader	
Guardian of Souls with Nightmare Lantern	1	1	140	Leader	
Knight of Shrouds	1	1	120	Leader	
Knight of Shrouds on Ethereal Steed	1	1	140	Leader	
Kurdoss Valentian, the Craven King	1	1	220	Leader	Unique
Lady Olynder, Mortarch of Grief	1	1	240	Leader	Unique
Lord Executioner	1	1	80	Leader	
Reikenor the Grimhailer	1	1	180	Leader	Unique
Spirit Torment	1	1	120	Leader	
Tomb Banshee	1	1	80	Leader	
Bladegheist Revenants	5	20	90/320		
Chainghasts	2	4	80		
Dreadscythe Harridans	5	20	90/320		
Glaivewraith Stalkers	4	16	60		
Grimghast Reapers	10	30	140/360		Battleline in Nighthaunt army
Hexwraiths	5	20	160		Battleline in Nighthaunt army
Myrmourn Banshees	4	12	80/210		
Spirit Hosts	3	12	120		Battleline in Nighthaunt army
Chainguard	-	-	*120*	*Warscroll Battalion*	
The Condemned	-	-	*150*	*Warscroll Battalion*	
Death Stalkers	-	-	*120*	*Warscroll Battalion*	
Deathriders	-	-	*130*	*Warscroll Battalion*	
Execution Horde	-	-	*100*	*Warscroll Battalion*	
Nighthaunt Procession	-	-	*80*	*Warscroll Battalion*	
Shrieker Host	-	-	*140*	*Warscroll Battalion*	
Shroudguard	-	-	*110*	*Warscroll Battalion*	
Mortalis Terminexus	*1*	*1*	*60*	*Endless Spell*	
Shyish Reaper	*1*	*1*	*40*	*Endless Spell*	
Vault of Souls	*1*	*1*	*40*	*Endless Spell*	

DEATH	ALLIES
Nighthaunt	Deathlords, Soulblight
Flesh-eater Courts	Deadwalkers, Deathlords, Deathmages
Grand Host of Nagash	Flesh-eater Courts, Nighthaunt
Legion of Blood	Flesh-eater Courts, Nighthaunt
Legion of Night	Flesh-eater Courts, Nighthaunt
Legion of Sacrament	Flesh-eater Courts, Nighthaunt
Soulblight	Deadwalkers, Deathlords, Deathmages, Deathrattle, Nighthaunt

DESTRUCTION PITCHED BATTLE PROFILES

ALEGUZZLER GARGANTS UNIT	UNIT SIZE MIN	UNIT SIZE MAX	POINTS	BATTLEFIELD ROLE	NOTES
✳ Aleguzzler Gargant	1	1	160	Behemoth	

BEASTCLAW RAIDERS UNIT	UNIT SIZE MIN	UNIT SIZE MAX	POINTS	BATTLEFIELD ROLE	NOTES
✳ Stonehorn Beastriders	1	1	320	Behemoth	Battleline, Behemoth in Beastclaw Raiders army
✳ Thundertusk Beastriders	1	1	340	Behemoth	Battleline, Behemoth in Beastclaw Raiders army
Icebrow Hunter	1	1	140	Leader	
✳ Frostlord on Stonehorn	1	1	420	Leader, Behemoth	
✳ Frostlord on Thundertusk	1	1	420	Leader, Behemoth	
✳ Huskard on Stonehorn	1	1	340	Leader, Behemoth	
✳ Huskard on Thundertusk	1	1	360	Leader, Behemoth	
Frost Sabres	2	12	40		Battleline in Beastclaw Raiders army if general is an Icebrow Hunter
✳ Icefall Yhetees	3	12	120		Battleline in Beastclaw Raiders army if general is mounted on a Thundertusk
Mournfang Pack	2	12	160		Battleline in Beastclaw Raiders army
✳ Alfrostun	-	-	100	Warscroll Battalion	
✳ Braggoth's Beast Hammer	-	-	230	Warscroll Battalion	
✳ Eurlbad	-	-	170	Warscroll Battalion	
✳ Jorlbad	-	-	160	Warscroll Battalion	
✳ Olwyr Alfrostun	-	-	190	Warscroll Battalion	
✳ Skal	-	-	150	Warscroll Battalion	
✳ Svard Alfrostun	-	-	150	Warscroll Battalion	
✳ Torrbad	-	-	170	Warscroll Battalion	

BONESPLITTERZ UNIT	UNIT SIZE MIN	MAX	POINTS	BATTLEFIELD ROLE	NOTES
Savage Orruks	10	30	120/300	Battleline	
Maniak Weirdnob	1	1	120	Leader	
Savage Big Boss	1	1	120	Leader	
Wardokk	1	1	100	Leader	
Wurrgog Prophet	1	1	140	Leader	
Savage Big Stabbas	2	8	100		
✷ Savage Boarboy Maniaks	5	20	140		Battleline in Bonesplitterz army
✷ Savage Boarboys	5	20	100		Battleline in Bonesplitterz army
✷ Savage Orruk Arrowboys	10	30	140		Battleline in Bonesplitterz army
Savage Orruk Morboys	10	30	120/300		Battleline in Bonesplitterz army
✷ Bonegrinz Warclan	-	-	110	Warscroll Battalion	
✷ Brutal Rukk	-	-	160	Warscroll Battalion	
✷ Drakkfoot Warclan	-	-	140	Warscroll Battalion	
✷ Icebone Warclan	-	-	160	Warscroll Battalion	
Kop Rukk	-	-	200	Warscroll Battalion	
✷ Kunnin' Rukk	-	-	200	Warscroll Battalion	
✷ Savage Warclan	-	-	80	Warscroll Battalion	
✷ Snaga Rukk	-	-	170	Warscroll Battalion	
✷ Teef Rukk	-	-	100	Warscroll Battalion	

FIREBELLIES UNIT	UNIT SIZE MIN	MAX	POINTS	BATTLEFIELD ROLE	NOTES
✷ Firebelly	1	1	120	Leader	

GITMOB GROTS UNIT	UNIT SIZE MIN	MAX	POINTS	BATTLEFIELD ROLE	NOTES
Doom Diver Catapult	1	1	120	Artillery	
Grot Rock Lobber	1	1	100	Artillery	
Grot Spear Chukka	1	1	120	Artillery	
Grots	20	60	100/270	Battleline	
Grot Shaman	1	1	80	Leader	
Grot Wolf Chariots	1	6	40		Battleline in Gitmob army
✷ Grot Wolf Riders	5	30	90/480		Battleline in Gitmob army
Nasty Skulkers	3	9	40		
Snotling Pump Wagons	1	3	60		
Snotlings	2	10	40		

GREENSKINZ UNIT	UNIT SIZE MIN	MAX	POINTS	BATTLEFIELD ROLE	NOTES
✷ Orruks	10	40	80/280	Battleline	
Orruk Great Shaman	1	1	120	Leader	
Orruk Warboss	1	1	140	Leader	
Orruk Warboss on Wyvern	1	1	240	Leader, Behemoth	
Orruk Boarboys	5	20	100/360		Battleline in Greenskinz army
Orruk Boar Chariots	1	3	80		Battleline in Greenskinz army

GUTBUSTERS UNIT	UNIT SIZE MIN	MAX	POINTS	BATTLEFIELD ROLE	NOTES
✳ Grot Scraplauncher	1	1	120	Artillery	
✳ Ironblaster	1	1	120	Artillery	
Ogors	3	12	120/400	Battleline	
Butcher	1	1	140	Leader	
Tyrant	1	1	160	Leader	
Gorgers	1	3	60		
Grots	20	60	100/270		
✳ Ironguts	3	12	180		Battleline in Gutbusters army
Leadbelchers	3	12	140		Battleline in Gutbusters army

IRONJAWZ UNIT	UNIT SIZE MIN	MAX	POINTS	BATTLEFIELD ROLE	NOTES
Orruk Megaboss	1	1	140	Leader	
Orruk Warchanter	1	1	80	Leader	
Orruk Weirdnob Shaman	1	1	120	Leader	
✳ Gordrakk, the Fist of Gork	1	1	580	Leader, Behemoth	Unique
✳ Megaboss on Maw-krusha	1	1	440	Leader, Behemoth	
✳ Orruk Ardboys	10	30	160/450		Battleline in Ironjawz army
Orruk Brutes	5	20	180		Battleline in Ironjawz army
Orruk Gore-gruntas	3	12	140		Battleline in Ironjawz army
✳ Ardfist	-	-	170	Warscroll Battalion	
✳ Bloodtoofs	-	-	120	Warscroll Battalion	
✳ Brawl	-	-	180	Warscroll Battalion	
Brutefist	-	-	180	Warscroll Battalion	
✳ Gorefist	-	-	190	Warscroll Battalion	
✳ Ironfist	-	-	180	Warscroll Battalion	
Ironsunz	-	-	120	Warscroll Battalion	
✳ Weirdfist	-	-	180	Warscroll Battalion	

MANEATERS UNIT	UNIT SIZE MIN	MAX	POINTS	BATTLEFIELD ROLE	NOTES
✳ Maneaters	3	12	200		

MOONCLAN GROTS UNIT	UNIT SIZE MIN	MAX	POINTS	BATTLEFIELD ROLE	NOTES
Grots	20	60	130/360	Battleline	
Mangler Squigs	1	1	240	Behemoth	
Grot Shaman	1	1	80	Leader	
✳ Grot Warboss	1	1	100	Leader	
✳ Grot Warboss on Great Cave Squig	1	1	100	Leader	
Cave Squigs	5	20	60		Battleline in Moonclan army
Fungoid Cave-Shaman	1	1	80	Leader	
Grot Fanatics	3	6	100		
Grot Squig Herders	2	10	20		
Grot Squig Hoppers	5	20	80		Battleline in Moonclan army

SPIDERFANG GROTS	UNIT SIZE		POINTS	BATTLEFIELD ROLE	NOTES
UNIT	MIN	MAX			
Arachnarok Spider	1	1	280	Behemoth	Leader, Behemoth if carrying a Spiderfang Grot Shaman
Grot Big Boss on Gigantic Spider	1	1	100	Leader	
Grot Spider Riders	5	30	100/540		Battleline in Spiderfang army

TROGGOTHS	UNIT SIZE		POINTS	BATTLEFIELD ROLE	NOTES
UNIT	MIN	MAX			
✱ Fellwater Troggoths	3	12	160		
✱ Rockgut Troggoths	3	12	160		
✱ Sourbreath Troggoths	3	12	160		

DESTRUCTION	ALLIES
Beastclaw Raiders	Aleguzzler Gargants, Firebellies, Gutbusters, Maneaters, Troggoths
Bonesplitterz	Aleguzzler Gargants, Greenskinz, Ironjawz, Moonclan Grots, Spiderfang Grots, Troggoths
Gitmob Grots	Aleguzzler Gargants, Greenskinz, Moonclan Grots, Spiderfang Grots, Troggoths
Greenskinz	Aleguzzler Gargants, Bonesplitterz, Gitmob Grots, Ironjawz, Moonclan Grots, Spiderfang Grots, Troggoths
Gutbusters	Aleguzzler Gargants, Beastclaw Raiders, Firebellies, Maneaters, Troggoths
Ironjawz	Aleguzzler Gargants, Bonesplitterz, Gitmob Grots, Greenskinz, Moonclan Grots, Troggoths
Moonclan Grots	Aleguzzler Gargants, Gitmob Grots, Greenskinz, Spiderfang Grots, Troggoths
Spiderfang Grots	Aleguzzler Gargants, Gitmob Grots, Greenskinz, Moonclan Grots, Troggoths

ORDER PITCHED BATTLE PROFILES

AELF UNIT	UNIT SIZE MIN	MAX	POINTS	BATTLEFIELD ROLE	NOTES
✳ Mistweaver Saih	1	1	100	Leader	
Tenebrael Shard	1	1	120	Leader	

COLLEGIATE ARCANE UNIT	UNIT SIZE MIN	MAX	POINTS	BATTLEFIELD ROLE	NOTES
Celestial Hurricanum	1	1	380	Behemoth	Leader, Behemoth if carrying Celestial Battlemage
Luminark of Hysh	1	1	240	Behemoth	Leader, Behemoth if carrying White Battlemage
✳ Battlemage	1	1	120	Leader	
✳ Battlemage on Griffon	1	1	240	Leader, Behemoth	
✳ War Council	-	-	180	Warscroll Battalion	

DARKLING COVENS UNIT	UNIT SIZE MIN	MAX	POINTS	BATTLEFIELD ROLE	NOTES
Bleakswords	10	40	100/360	Battleline	
Darkshards	10	40	100	Battleline	
Dreadspears	10	40	100/360	Battleline	
✳ Sorceress	1	1	100	Leader	
✳ Sorceress on Black Dragon	1	1	280	Leader, Behemoth	
✳ Black Guard	10	30	140/360		Battleline in Darkling Covens army
✳ Executioners	10	30	160/420		Battleline in Darkling Covens army
Thrall Warhost	-	-	180	Warscroll Battalion	

DAUGHTERS OF KHAINE UNIT	UNIT SIZE MIN	MAX	POINTS	BATTLEFIELD ROLE	NOTES
Sisters of Slaughter	10	30	120/300	Battleline	
Witch Aelves	10	30	100/270	Battleline	
Avatar of Khaine	1	1	180	Behemoth	
Bloodwrack Medusa	1	1	140	Leader	
Hag Queen	1	1	60	Leader	
Morathi, High Oracle of Khaine	1	1	480	Leader	Unique. Can transform into Morathi, the Shadow Queen during battle
Slaughter Queen	1	1	100	Leader	
Bloodwrack Shrine	1	1	220	Leader, Behemoth	
Hag Queen on Cauldron of Blood	1	1	300	Leader, Behemoth	
Slaughter Queen on Cauldron of Blood	1	1	330	Leader, Behemoth	
Doomfire Warlocks	5	20	160		
Blood Sisters	5	20	140/480		Battleline in Daughters of Khaine army if general is a **BLOODWRACK MEDUSA**
Blood Stalkers	5	20	160		
Khinerai Heartrenders	5	20	80		
Khinerai Lifetakers	5	20	80/280		
✳ *Cauldron Guard*	-	-	*120*	*Warscroll Battalion*	
✳ *Temple Nest*	-	-	*130*	*Warscroll Battalion*	
✳ *Shadow Patrol*	-	-	*130*	*Warscroll Battalion*	
✳ *Shadowhammer Compact*	-	-	*170*	*Warscroll Battalion*	
✳ *Slaughter Troupe*	-	-	*130*	*Warscroll Battalion*	
War Coven of Morathi	-	-	*100*	*Warscroll Battalion*	

DEVOTED OF SIGMAR UNIT	UNIT SIZE MIN	MAX	POINTS	BATTLEFIELD ROLE	NOTES
Excelsior Warpriest	1	1	80	Leader	
Warrior Priest	1	1	80	Leader	
✳ Witch Hunter	1	1	50	Leader	
War Altar of Sigmar	1	1	250	Leader, Behemoth	
Flagellants	10	40	80/260		Battleline in Devoted of Sigmar army
✳ *Pilgrimage of Wrath*	-	-	*140*	*Warscroll Battalion*	

DISPOSSESSED UNIT	UNIT SIZE MIN	MAX	POINTS	BATTLEFIELD ROLE	NOTES
Warriors	10	40	80/280	Battleline	
✳ Longbeards	10	30	100/270	Battleline	
✳ Runelord	1	1	100	Leader	
Unforged	1	1	100	Leader	
Warden King	1	1	120	Leader	
✳ Hammerers	10	30	160/420		Battleline in Dispossessed army
✳ Ironbreakers	10	30	140/360		Battleline in Dispossessed army
✳ Irondrakes	10	30	180		
Quarrellers	10	30	120		
Thunderers	10	30	120		
✳ *Grudgebound War Throng*	-	-	*170*	*Warscroll Battalion*	

ELDRITCH COUNCIL UNIT	UNIT SIZE MIN	MAX	POINTS	BATTLEFIELD ROLE	NOTES
✱ Archmage	1	1	100	Leader	
✱ Loremaster	1	1	140	Leader	
Archmage on Dragon	1	1	320	Leader, Behemoth	
Drakeseer	1	1	300	Leader, Behemoth	
✱ Swordmasters	10	30	160/420		Battleline in Eldritch Council army

FREE PEOPLES UNIT	UNIT SIZE MIN	MAX	POINTS	BATTLEFIELD ROLE	NOTES
Freeguild Archers	10	30	100	Battleline	
Freeguild Crossbowmen	10	30	100	Battleline	
Freeguild Guard	10	40	80/280	Battleline	
Freeguild Handgunners	10	30	100	Battleline	
Freeguild General	1	1	100	Leader	
Freeguild General on Griffon	1	1	260	Leader, Behemoth	
✱ Demigryph Knights	3	12	140		Battleline in Free Peoples army
✱ Freeguild Greatswords	10	30	140/360		Battleline in Free Peoples army
Freeguild Outriders	5	20	130		
Freeguild Pistoliers	5	20	130		
✱ Freeguild Regiment	-	-	210	Warscroll Battalion	

FYRESLAYERS UNIT	UNIT SIZE MIN	MAX	POINTS	BATTLEFIELD ROLE	NOTES
✱ Vulkite Berzerkers	10	30	120	Battleline	
✱ Auric Runefather	1	1	100	Leader	
Auric Runemaster	1	1	80	Leader	
✱ Auric Runesmiter	1	1	120	Leader	
Auric Runeson	1	1	80	Leader	
✱ Battlesmith	1	1	120	Leader	
Doomseeker	1	1	80	Leader	
Grimwrath Berzerker	1	1	80	Leader	
Auric Runefather on Magmadroth	1	1	260	Leader, Behemoth	
Auric Runesmiter on Magmadroth	1	1	200	Leader, Behemoth	
Auric Runeson on Magmadroth	1	1	240	Leader, Behemoth	
Auric Hearthguard	5	30	100/480		Battleline in Fyreslayers army if general is an Auric Runemaster
Hearthguard Berzerkers	5	30	100/480		Battleline in Fyreslayers army if general is an AURIC RUNEFATHER
✱ Forge Brethren	-	-	140	Warscroll Battalion	
✱ Grand Fyrd	-	-	60	Warscroll Battalion	
✱ Greyfyrd Lodge	-	-	60	Warscroll Battalion	
✱ Lords of the Lodge	-	-	110	Warscroll Battalion	
✱ Warrior Kinband	-	-	120	Warscroll Battalion	
✱ Vostarg Lodge	-	-	100	Warscroll Battalion	

IRONWELD ARSENAL UNIT	UNIT SIZE MIN	MAX	POINTS	BATTLEFIELD ROLE	NOTES
✶ Cannon	1	1	160	Artillery	
Helblaster Volley Gun	1	1	120	Artillery	
Helstorm Rocket Battery	1	1	180	Artillery	
Organ Gun	1	1	120	Artillery	
✶ Steam Tank	1	1	260	Behemoth	
Cogsmith	1	1	100	Leader	
Gunmaster	1	1	80	Leader	
Gyrobombers	1	1	80		
Gyrocopters	1	1	80		
✶ Artillery Detachment	-	-	120	Warscroll Battalion	

IDONETH DEEPKIN UNIT	UNIT SIZE MIN	MAX	POINTS	BATTLEFIELD ROLE	NOTES
Namarti Thralls	10	30	140/360	Battleline	
Akhelian Leviadon	1	1	380	Behemoth	
Volturnos, High King of the Deep	1	1	280	Leader	Unique
Eidolon of Mathlann, Aspect of the Storm	1	1	400	Leader	
Eidolon of Mathlann, Aspect of the Sea	1	1	440	Leader	
Akhelian King	1	1	240	Leader	
Isharann Tidecaster	1	1	100	Leader	
Isharann Soulrender	1	1	100	Leader	
Isharann Soulscryer	1	1	100	Leader	
Lotann, Warden of the Soul Ledgers	1	1	100	Leader	Unique
Akhelian Allopex	1	4	140		
Akhelian Ishlaen Guard	3	12	140		Battleline in Idoneth Deepkin army if general is an AKHELIAN HERO
Akhelian Morrsarr Guard	3	12	160		Battleline in Idoneth Deepkin army if general is an AKHELIAN HERO
Namarti Reavers	10	20	140		Battleline in Idoneth Deepkin army if general is an ISHARANN HERO
Alliance of Wood and Sea	-	-	140	Warscroll Battalion	
Akhelian Corps	-	-	100	Warscroll Battalion	
Namarti Corps	-	-	100	Warscroll Battalion	
Phalanx	-	-	120	Warscroll Battalion	
Royal Council	-	-	140	Warscroll Battalion	
Gloomtide Shipwreck	1	1	0	Scenery	

KHARADRON OVERLORDS UNIT	UNIT SIZE MIN	MAX	POINTS	BATTLEFIELD ROLE	NOTES
✹ Grundstok Gunhauler	1	1	160	Artillery	
Arkanaut Company	10	40	120	Battleline	
✹ Arkanaut Frigate	1	1	240	Behemoth	
✹ Arkanaut Ironclad	1	1	420	Behemoth	
✹ Aether-Khemist	1	1	160	Leader	
✹ Aetheric Navigator	1	1	80	Leader	
✹ Arkanaut Admiral	1	1	120	Leader	
✹ Brokk Grungsson, Lord-Magnate of Barak-Nar	1	1	260	Leader	Unique
✹ Endrinmaster	1	1	120	Leader	
Endrinriggers	3	12	120		
Grundstok Thunderers	5	20	100		
✹ Skywardens	3	12	120		
✹ *Aetherstrike Force*	-	-	*150*	*Warscroll Battalion*	
✹ *Grand Armada*	-	-	*100*	*Warscroll Battalion*	
✹ *Grundstok Escort Wing*	-	-	*130*	*Warscroll Battalion*	
✹ *Iron Sky Command*	-	-	*150*	*Warscroll Battalion*	
✹ *Iron Sky Squadron*	-	-	*130*	*Warscroll Battalion*	

LION RANGERS UNIT	UNIT SIZE MIN	MAX	POINTS	BATTLEFIELD ROLE	NOTES
✹ White Lion Chariots	1	3	80		
✹ White Lions	10	30	120/300		

ORDER DRACONIS UNIT	UNIT SIZE MIN	MAX	POINTS	BATTLEFIELD ROLE	NOTES
Dragon Noble	1	1	100	Leader	
Dragonlord	1	1	340	Leader, Behemoth	
Dragon Blades	5	20	140		Battleline in Order Draconis army
✹ *Dragonlord Host*	-	-	*130*	*Warscroll Battalion*	

ORDER SERPENTIS UNIT	UNIT SIZE MIN	MAX	POINTS	BATTLEFIELD ROLE	NOTES
✹ War Hydra	1	1	180	Behemoth	
Dreadlord on Black Dragon	1	1	320	Leader, Behemoth	
✹ Drakespawn Chariots	1	3	80		Battleline in Order Serpentis army
✹ Drakespawn Knights	5	20	140		Battleline in Order Serpentis army
✹ *Ebondrake Warhost*	-	-	*150*	*Warscroll Battalion*	

PHOENIX TEMPLE UNIT	UNIT SIZE MIN	MAX	POINTS	BATTLEFIELD ROLE	NOTES
✹ Flamespyre Phoenix	1	1	380	Behemoth	Leader, Behemoth if ridden by an Anointed
✹ Frostheart Phoenix	1	1	280	Behemoth	Leader, Behemoth if ridden by an Anointed
Anointed	1	1	80	Leader	
✹ Phoenix Guard	10	30	140/360		Battleline in Phoenix Temple army
✹ *Spyreheart Warhost*	-	-	*130*	*Warscroll Battalion*	

SCOURGE PRIVATEERS UNIT	UNIT SIZE MIN	MAX	POINTS	BATTLEFIELD ROLE	NOTES
✳ Kharibdyss	1	1	160	Behemoth	
Black Ark Fleetmaster	1	1	40	Leader	
Black Ark Corsairs	10	40	80/260		Battleline in Scourge Privateers army
✳ Scourgerunner Chariots	1	3	80		Battleline in Scourge Privateers army
✳ *Realm Reavers*	-	-	*150*	*Warscroll Battalion*	

SERAPHON UNIT	UNIT SIZE MIN	MAX	POINTS	BATTLEFIELD ROLE	NOTES
Razordons	1	4	40	Artillery	
Salamanders	1	4	40	Artillery	
Saurus Warriors	10	40	100/360	Battleline	
Bastiladon	1	1	280	Behemoth	
✳ Stegadon	1	1	220	Behemoth	
✳ Troglodon	1	1	160	Behemoth	
Lord Kroak	1	1	450	Leader	Unique
Saurus Astrolith Bearer	1	1	160	Leader	
Saurus Eternity Warden	1	1	140	Leader	
Saurus Oldblood	1	1	120	Leader	
Saurus Scar-Veteran on Cold One	1	1	100	Leader	
Saurus Sunblood	1	1	120	Leader	
Skink Priest	1	1	80	Leader	
Skink Starpriest	1	1	80	Leader	
Skink Starseer	1	1	200	Leader	
Slann Starmaster	1	1	260	Leader	
Engine of the Gods	1	1	220	Leader, Behemoth	
✳ Saurus Oldblood on Carnosaur	1	1	260	Leader, Behemoth	
Saurus Scar-Veteran on Carnosaur	1	1	240	Leader, Behemoth	
Chameleon Skinks	5	20	120		
Kroxigor	3	12	160		
Ripperdactyl Riders	3	12	140		
✳ Saurus Guard	5	20	90		Battleline in Seraphon army
✳ Saurus Knights	5	20	90		Battleline in Seraphon army
Skink Handlers	3	12	40		
✳ Skinks	10	40	60		Battleline in Seraphon army
Terradon Riders	3	12	120		
✳ *Bloodclaw Starhost*	-	-	*150*	*Warscroll Battalion*	
✳ *Dracothion's Tail*	-	-	*80*	*Warscroll Battalion*	
✳ *Eternal Starhost*	-	-	*150*	*Warscroll Battalion*	
✳ *Fangs of Sotek*	-	-	*70*	*Warscroll Battalion*	
✳ *Firelance Starhost*	-	-	*150*	*Warscroll Battalion*	
✳ *Heavenswatch Starhost*	-	-	*180*	*Warscroll Battalion*	
✳ *Shadowstrike Starhost*	-	-	*180*	*Warscroll Battalion*	
✳ *Starbeast Constellation*	-	-	*70*	*Warscroll Battalion*	
Sunclaw Starhost	-	-	*130*	*Warscroll Battalion*	
✳ *Thunderquake Starhost*	-	-	*120*	*Warscroll Battalion*	

SHADOWBLADES UNIT	UNIT SIZE MIN	MAX	POINTS	BATTLEFIELD ROLE	NOTES
Assassin	1	1	80	Leader	
Dark Riders	5	20	120		Battleline in Shadowblades army

STORMCAST ETERNALS UNIT	UNIT SIZE MIN	MAX	POINTS	BATTLEFIELD ROLE	NOTES
Celestar Ballista	1	1	100	Artillery	
Liberators	5	30	100/520	Battleline	
Astreia Solbright	1	1	220	Leader	Unique
Aventis Firestrike, Magister of Hammerhal	1	1	360	Leader	Unique
Celestant-Prime, Hammer of Sigmar	1	1	340	Leader	Unique
Gavriel Sureheart	1	1	100	Leader	Unique
✹ Knight-Azyros	1	1	100	Leader	
✹ Knight-Heraldor	1	1	100	Leader	
Knight-Incantor	1	1	140	Leader	
Knight-Questor	1	1	100	Leader	
Knight-Venator	1	1	120	Leader	
✹ Knight-Vexillor	1	1	120	Leader	
Knight-Zephyros	1	1	100	Leader	
Lord-Aquilor	1	1	200	Leader	
Lord-Arcanum	1	1	180	Leader	
Lord-Arcanum on Tauralon	1	1	340	Leader	
Lord-Arcanum on Dracoline	1	1	240	Leader	
Lord-Arcanum on Gryph-charger	1	1	240	Leader	
Lord-Castellant	1	1	100	Leader	
Lord-Celestant	1	1	100	Leader	
Lord-Celestant on Dracoth	1	1	220	Leader	
Lord-Exorcist	1	1	140	Leader	
✹ Lord-Ordinator	1	1	140	Leader	
✹ Lord-Relictor	1	1	100	Leader	
Lord-Veritant	1	1	120	Leader	
Neave Blacktalon	1	1	120	Leader	Unique
Vandus Hammerhand	1	1	280	Leader	Unique
✹ Drakesworn Templar	1	1	460	Leader, Behemoth	
Lord-Celestant on Stardrake	1	1	560	Leader, Behemoth	
✹ Aetherwings	3	12	50		
Castigators	3	18	80		
✹ Concussors	2	12	260		
Decimators	5	20	200		
✹ Desolators	2	12	220		
Evocators	5	20	200		
Evocators on Dracolines	3	12	300		
The Farstriders	3	3	100		Unique
Fulminators	2	12	240		
✹ Gryph-hounds	6	18	140		
Judicators	5	20	160		Battleline in Stormcast Eternal army
Prosecutors	3	12	100		
Protectors	5	20	200		

STORMCAST ETERNALS UNIT	UNIT SIZE MIN	MAX	POINTS	BATTLEFIELD ROLE	NOTES
Retributors	5	20	220		
Sequitors	5	20	120/400		Battleline in Stormcast Eternal army if general is a **LORD-ARCANUM**
Steelheart's Champions	3	3	100		Unique
Tempestors	2	12	220		
✷ Vanguard-Hunters	5	15	120		Battleline in Stormcast Eternal army if general is a Lord-Aquilor
✷ Vanguard-Palladors	3	12	200		
✷ Vanguard-Raptors with Hurricane Crossbows	3	12	140		
Vanguard-Raptors with Longstrike Crossbows	3	12	180		
Cleansing Phalanx	-	-	120	Warscroll Battalion	
✷ Devastation Brotherhood	-	-	110	Warscroll Battalion	
✷ Drakesworn Temple	-	-	140	Warscroll Battalion	
✷ Exemplar Chamber	-	-	80	Warscroll Battalion	
✷ Extremis Chamber	-	-	100	Warscroll Battalion	
Grand Convocation	-	-	130	Warscroll Battalion	
Hailstorm Battery	-	-	120	Warscroll Battalion	
✷ Hammerstrike Force	-	-	120	Warscroll Battalion	
✷ Harbinger Chamber	-	-	100	Warscroll Battalion	
✷ Lightning Echelon	-	-	130	Warscroll Battalion	
✷ Lords of the Storm	-	-	140	Warscroll Battalion	
Sacrosanct Chamber	-	-	70	Warscroll Battalion	
✷ Skyborne Slayers	-	-	190	Warscroll Battalion	
Soulstrike Brotherhood	-	-	120	Warscroll Battalion	
✷ Thunderhead Brotherhood	-	-	160	Warscroll Battalion	
✷ Thunderwave Echelon	-	-	100	Warscroll Battalion	
✷ Vanguard Angelos Conclave	-	-	160	Warscroll Battalion	
✷ Vanguard Auxiliary Chamber	-	-	160	Warscroll Battalion	
✷ Vanguard Justicar Conclave	-	-	120	Warscroll Battalion	
✷ Vanguard Wing	-	-	140	Warscroll Battalion	
✷ Warrior Brotherhood	-	-	180	Warscroll Battalion	
✷ Warrior Chamber	-	-	80	Warscroll Battalion	
Celestian Vortex	1	1	40	Endless Spell	
Dais Arcanum	1	1	40	Endless Spell	
Everblaze Comet	1	1	100	Endless Spell	

SWIFTHAWK AGENTS UNIT	UNIT SIZE MIN	MAX	POINTS	BATTLEFIELD ROLE	NOTES
✷ Reavers	5	20	140	Battleline	
Skywarden	1	1	160	Leader	
High Warden	1	1	220	Leader, Behemoth	
Chariots	1	3	80		
✷ Shadow Warriors	10	30	180		Battleline in Swifthawk Agents army
Skycutters	1	3	120		
Spireguard	10	30	120/300		Battleline in Swifthawk Agents army

SYLVANETH UNIT	UNIT SIZE MIN	UNIT SIZE MAX	POINTS	BATTLEFIELD ROLE	NOTES
Dryads	10	30	100/270	Battleline	
Treelord	1	1	240	Behemoth	
Branchwraith	1	1	80	Leader	
Branchwych	1	1	80	Leader	
Alarielle the Everqueen	1	1	600	Leader, Behemoth	Unique
Drycha Hamadreth	1	1	280	Leader, Behemoth	Unique
❋ Spirit of Durthu	1	1	380	Leader, Behemoth	
Treelord Ancient	1	1	300	Leader, Behemoth	
❋ Kurnoth Hunters	3	12	200		
❋ Spite-Revenants	5	30	70/360		Battleline in Sylvaneth army
Tree-Revenants	5	30	80/420		Battleline in Sylvaneth army
❋ Dreadwood Wargrove	-	-	90	*Warscroll Battalion*	
❋ Forest Folk	-	-	140	*Warscroll Battalion*	
❋ Forest Spirit Wargrove	-	-	140	*Warscroll Battalion*	
❋ Free Spirits	-	-	120	*Warscroll Battalion*	
❋ Gnarlroot Wargrove	-	-	130	*Warscroll Battalion*	
❋ The Guardians of Alarielle	-	-	200	*Warscroll Battalion*	
❋ Harvestboon Wargrove	-	-	100	*Warscroll Battalion*	
❋ Heartwood Wargrove	-	-	80	*Warscroll Battalion*	
❋ Household	-	-	100	*Warscroll Battalion*	
❋ Ironbark Wargrove	-	-	80	*Warscroll Battalion*	
❋ Lords of the Clan	-	-	100	*Warscroll Battalion*	
❋ Oakenbrow Wargrove	-	-	90	*Warscroll Battalion*	
Outcasts	-	-	90	*Warscroll Battalion*	
❋ Sylvaneth Wargrove	-	-	80	*Warscroll Battalion*	
❋ Winterleaf Wargrove	-	-	90	*Warscroll Battalion*	
Sylvaneth Wyldwood	1	1	0	*Scenery*	*Each Sylvaneth Wyldwood is comprised of 1-3 Citadel Woods*

WANDERERS UNIT	UNIT SIZE MIN	UNIT SIZE MAX	POINTS	BATTLEFIELD ROLE	NOTES
Glade Guard	10	30	120	Battleline	
Nomad Prince	1	1	80	Leader	
❋ Spellweaver	1	1	100	Leader	
Wayfinder	1	1	100	Leader	
Waystrider	1	1	80	Leader	
❋ Waywatcher	1	1	120	Leader	
❋ Eternal Guard	10	30	70		Battleline in Wanderer army
Sisters of the Thorn	5	20	220		
❋ Sisters of the Watch	10	30	180		Battleline in Wanderer army if general is a Waywatcher
❋ Wild Riders	5	20	120		
❋ Wildwood Rangers	10	30	140		Battleline in Wanderer army if general is a Wayfinder
❋ Waystone Pathfinders	-	-	200	*Warscroll Battalion*	

ORDER	ALLIES
Darkling Covens	Daughters of Khaine, Idoneth Deepkin, Order Serpentis, Scourge Privateers, Shadowblades, Stormcast Eternals
Daughters of Khaine	Darkling Covens, Idoneth Deepkin, Order Serpentis, Scourge Privateers, Shadowblades, Stormcast Eternals
Devoted of Sigmar	Collegiate Arcane, Free Peoples, Ironweld Arsenal, Stormcast Eternals
Dispossessed	Fyreslayers, Ironweld Arsenal, Kharadron Overlords, Stormcast Eternals
Eldritch Council	Idoneth Deepkin, Lion Rangers, Order Draconis, Phoenix Temple, Stormcast Eternals, Swifthawk Agents, Sylvaneth, Wanderers
Free Peoples	Collegiate Arcane, Devoted of Sigmar, Ironweld Arsenal, Stormcast Eternals
Fyreslayers	Dispossessed, Ironweld Arsenal, Kharadron Overlords, Stormcast Eternals
Idoneth Deepkin	Darkling Covens, Daughters of Khaine, Eldritch Council, Order Serpentis, Scourge Privateers, Shadowblades, Stormcast Eternals, Sylvaneth, Wanderers
Kharadron Overlords	Dispossessed, Fyreslayers, Ironweld Arsenal, Stormcast Eternals
Order Draconis	Eldritch Council, Lion Rangers, Phoenix Temple, Stormcast Eternals, Swifthawk Agents, Sylvaneth, Wanderers
Order Serpentis	Darkling Covens, Daughters of Khaine, Idoneth Deepkin, Scourge Privateers, Shadowblades, Stormcast Eternals
Phoenix Temple	Eldritch Council, Lion Rangers, Order Draconis, Stormcast Eternals, Swifthawk Agents, Sylvaneth, Wanderers
Scourge Privateers	Darkling Covens, Daughters of Khaine, Idoneth Deepkin, Order Serpentis, Shadowblades, Stormcast Eternals
Seraphon	Stormcast Eternals
Shadowblades	Darkling Covens, Daughters of Khaine, Idoneth Deepkin, Order Serpentis, Scourge Privateers, Stormcast Eternals
Stormcast Eternals	Any ORDER faction
Swifthawk Agents	Eldritch Council, Lion Rangers, Order Draconis, Phoenix Temple, Stormcast Eternals, Sylvaneth, Wanderers
Sylvaneth	Idoneth Deepkin, Stormcast Eternals, Wanderers
Wanderers	Eldritch Council, Idoneth Deepkin, Lion Rangers, Order Draconis, Phoenix Temple, Stormcast Eternals, Swifthawk Agents, Sylvaneth

ADDITIONAL PITCHED BATTLE PROFILES

Designer's Note: *The following section lists publications that feature units from more than one Grand Alliance.*

BLIGHTWAR UNIT	UNIT SIZE MIN	MAX	POINTS	BATTLEFIELD ROLE	NOTES
✴ Aetherwings	3	12	50		
Horticulous Slimux	1	1	220	Leader	Unique
Neave Blacktalon	1	1	120	Leader	Unique
Nurglings	3	12	100		
Plague Drones	3	12	200		
Plaguebearers	10	30	120/320	Battleline	
✴ Vanguard-Hunters	5	15	120		Battleline in Stormcast Eternal army if general is a Lord-Aquilor
✴ Vanguard-Palladors	3	12	200		
✴ Vanguard-Raptors with Hurricane Crossbows	3	12	140		
Vanguard-Raptors with Longstrike Crossbows	3	12	180		
Blacktalon's Shadowhammers	-	-	*160*	*Warscroll Battalion*	
Fecund Rituculturalists	-	-	*180*	*Warscroll Battalion*	

GENERAL'S HANDBOOK UNIT	UNIT SIZE MIN	MAX	POINTS	BATTLEFIELD ROLE	NOTES
✶ Bloodtoofs	-	-	120	Warscroll Battalion	
✶ Dracothion's Tail	-	-	80	Warscroll Battalion	
✶ Fangs of Sotek	-	-	70	Warscroll Battalion	
✶ Greyfyrd Lodge	-	-	60	Warscroll Battalion	
Ironsunz	-	-	120	Warscroll Battalion	
✶ Vostarg Lodge	-	-	100	Warscroll Battalion	

MALIGN PORTENTS UNIT	UNIT SIZE MIN	MAX	POINTS	BATTLEFIELD ROLE	NOTES
Darkoath Warqueen	1	1	80	Leader	
Fungoid Cave-Shaman	1	1	80	Leader	
Knight of Shrouds	1	1	120	Leader	
✶ Lord-Ordinator	1	1	140	Leader	

MALIGN SORCERY UNIT	UNIT SIZE MIN	MAX	POINTS	BATTLEFIELD ROLE	NOTES
Aethervoid Pendulum	1	1	40	Endless Spell	
Balewind Vortex	1	1	40	Endless Spell	
The Burning Head	1	1	40	Endless Spell	
Chronomantic Cogs	1	1	60	Endless Spell	
Emerald Lifeswarm	1	1	60	Endless Spell	
Geminids of Uhl-Gysh	1	1	40	Endless Spell	
Malevolent Maelstrom	1	1	20	Endless Spell	
Prismatic Palisade	1	1	30	Endless Spell	
Purple Sun of Shyish	1	1	100	Endless Spell	
Quicksilver Swords	1	1	20	Endless Spell	
Ravenak's Gnashing Jaws	1	1	40	Endless Spell	
Soulsnare Shackles	1	1	20	Endless Spell	
Suffocating Gravetide	1	1	30	Endless Spell	
Umbral Spellportal	1	1	60	Endless Spell	

WARHAMMER UNDERWORLDS: SHADESPIRE UNIT	UNIT SIZE MIN	MAX	POINTS	BATTLEFIELD ROLE	NOTES
The Chosen Axes	3	3	40		Unique. Cannot be taken unless army includes Fjul-Grimnir
The Farstriders	3	3	100		Unique
Fjul-Grimnir	1	1	100	Leader	Unique. Cannot be taken unless army includes the Chosen Axes
Garrek's Reavers	5	5	60		Unique
Ironskull's Boyz	4	4	80		Unique
Magore's Fiends	3	3	80		Unique. Cannot be taken unless army includes Riptooth
Riptooth	1	1	40		Unique. Cannot be taken unless army includes Magore's Fiends
The Sepulchral Guard	7	7	80		Unique
Skritch Spiteclaw	1	1	120	Leader	Unique. Cannot be taken unless army includes Spiteclaw's Swarm
Spiteclaw's Swarm	4	4	30		Unique. Cannot be taken unless army includes Skritch Spiteclaw
Steelheart's Champions	3	3	100		Unique

All across the Mortal Realms, mighty armies of warriors fight endless wars of conquest and destruction. In this section you will find updated sets of allegiance and summoning abilities for many of the factions that make up the four Grand Alliances. In addition, this section contains warscrolls for using Citadel Miniatures terrain features in your games, allowing you to augment the battlefield with arcane constructions and ancient edifices.

Using the rules in this section will help bring your battles to life. Scenery warscrolls enhance the experience of battling on the tabletop by allowing your armies to interact with terrain features in new and exciting ways. Some provide rules for buildings that, when garrisoned, bestow powerful abilities on the warriors or wizards within. Others turn the features of the Mortal Realms into hazardous obstacles with which your attacking soldiers must contend, or natural redoubts towards which your defenders can flock. Every Citadel scenery model has its own unique warscroll, which makes the process of selecting and setting up scenery before the start of a battle just as enjoyable and strategically important as the selection and deployment of your army.

Updated summoning abilities add even more excitement to your games, allowing you to raise unquiet grave spirits or draw daemonic entities into the fray. Whether through magic, prayer or the despoilment of the Mortal Realms themselves, these summoning abilities provide new and evocative ways to augment your army mid-battle.

The allegiance abilities in this section include battle traits, command traits and artefacts of power for a number of factions. These additional rules allow you to field armies that act and fight in the way they are described in the stories you have read about the Age of Sigmar. For example, a Skaven Pestilens army will spread disease and plague wherever it goes, while the duardin of the Dispossessed will dogmatically pursue their grudges until all who have slighted them are punished. The rules for using allegiance abilities can be found in the core rules.

If you are looking for even more tools to enhance your hobby and gaming experiences, Warhammer Age of Sigmar: The App is your indispensable companion to collecting and gaming in the Mortal Realms. With this app you can download or read books, quickly reference rules, access warscrolls and even build army lists. In addition, Warhammer TV provides painting tutorials that are available for free at games-workshop.com and via the Warhammer TV YouTube channel.

ARCANE RUIN

Many of the Arcane Ruins that dot the Mortal Realms date back to the Age of Myth.
Some were used in fell rituals or divine ceremonies, whereas others were constructed
to house artefacts of great power, or as tombs for mighty sorcerers.

DESCRIPTION

An Arcane Ruin is a single terrain feature. It is an obstacle.

SCENERY RULES

Site of Power: *These ancient ruins absorb magic out of the air itself, which can then be harnessed by a nearby wizard to empower their spell-casting.*

The Arcane scenery rule (see right) from the Scenery table must be used for this terrain feature.

Arcane: Add 1 to casting or unbinding rolls for **WIZARDS** while they are within 1" of any Arcane terrain features.

KEYWORDS	SCENERY, ARCANE RUIN

AZYRITE RUINS

During the Age of Myth, the Mortal Realms were populated with civilizations that
worshipped the pantheon of Azyr. Now, all that remains of their great cities and
magnificent temples are crumbling ruins.

DESCRIPTION

An Azyrite Ruin is a single terrain feature. It is an obstacle.

KEYWORDS	SCENERY, AZYRITE RUINS

BALEFUL REALMGATE

Where the powers of the Dark Gods have cursed a conduit through the Mortal Realms,
there stands a Baleful Realmgate, bathing the lands around it in unnatural light and
flickering with bizarre energies.

DESCRIPTION

A Baleful Realmgate is a single terrain feature. It is an obstacle.

SCENERY RULES

Spirit Journey: *Brave warriors can cross a Realmgate's threshold, emerging moments later from a different Realmgate nearby.*

At the start of your movement phase, you can use one Baleful Realmgate to transport one unit from your army. In order to do so, the unit must be wholly within 6" of the Baleful Realmgate, and a friendly **Wizard** or **Priest** must be within 6" of the Baleful Realmgate. If this is the case, remove the unit from the battlefield, and then set it up wholly within 6" of another Baleful Realmgate and more than 9" from any enemy models. This counts as that unit's move for that movement phase.

KEYWORDS	SCENERY, REALMGATE, BALEFUL REALMGATE

BARBED VENOMGORSE

Those straying too close to a patch of Barbed Venomgorse will find themselves
whipped with toxin-engorged pins that will render them paralytic while they are
slowly digested by the plant.

DESCRIPTION

A set of Barbed Venomgorse is a single terrain feature that consists of 3 Barbed Venomgorse models. These must be set up as a single group, with all models within 1" of at least one other model from the group. A set of Barbed Venomgorse is an obstacle.

SCENERY RULES

Cunning Sentience: *Possessed of a primal intelligence, this carnivorous plant is highly adaptable, and is able to generate new weapon-growths and toxins throughout its life cycle.*

The Deadly scenery rule (see right) from the Scenery table must be used for this terrain feature.

Deadly: Roll a dice for each unit that finishes a normal move or charge move within 1" of any Deadly terrain features. On a 1, that unit suffers D3 mortal wounds.

KEYWORDS	SCENERY, BARBED VENOMGORSE

CITADEL WOOD

Thick and tangled forests sprout in every realm, though the flora that makes up each varies wildly. From the lush copses of Ghyran to the withered deadwoods of Shyish, these woods shape many a battlefield.

DESCRIPTION

A Citadel Wood is a single terrain feature. It is an obstacle.

SCENERY RULES

Overgrown Wilderness: *It is only possible to see a few yards into these woodlands before visibility is blocked by the dense undergrowth.*

Models are not visible to each other if an imaginary straight line 1mm wide drawn between the closest points of the two models crosses over more than 1" of the base of a Citadel Wood. This scenery rule does not apply if either model can fly.

KEYWORDS	SCENERY, CITADEL WOOD

DRAGONFATE DAIS

Ringed with draconic carvings whose eyes glow with divine light, a Dragonfate Dais is a locus through which mortals can beseech the gods for aid. But there is always a price to be paid when invoking such power.

DESCRIPTION

A Dragonfate Dais is a single terrain feature. It is an obstacle.

SCENERY RULES

Beseech the Gods: *A Dragonfate Dais is an ancient site of power where those in desperate need are able to call upon the gods for aid.*

The Damned scenery rule (see right) from the Scenery table must be used for this terrain feature.

Damned: At the start of your hero phase, you can pick one friendly unit within 1" of a Damned terrain feature to make a sacrifice. If you do so, that unit suffers D3 mortal wounds, but you can re-roll hit rolls of 1 for it until your next hero phase.

KEYWORDS	SCENERY, DRAGONFATE DAIS

MAGEWRATH THRONE

Constructed in an ancient time by powerful and insane wizards, these mighty thrones are highly sought after as seats of power by warlords who wish to use the bound magic within to conquer their enemies.

DESCRIPTION

A Magewrath Throne is a single terrain feature. It is an obstacle.

SCENERY RULES

Ascend to the Throne: *A general who takes the throne can use the magic imbued within it to wreak wrath and ruin upon his enemies, amplifying the bravado and strength of his troops while demoralising and weakening the resolve of the foe.*

At the start of your hero phase, if your general is within 3" of any Magewrath Thrones and an enemy general is not, add 1 to the number of command points you receive that hero phase.

KEYWORDS	SCENERY, MAGEWRATH THRONE

NUMINOUS OCCULUM

Glimpses of events past and future are projected into the minds of those who behold a Numinous Occulum's arching astrolabes. The mindful can use these portents to protect incoming blows and defend against unseen attacks.

DESCRIPTION

A Numinous Occulum is a single terrain feature. It is an obstacle.

SCENERY RULES

Eldritch Energy: *Troops standing near to a Numinous Occulum gain a measure of protection against any harm.*

The Mystical scenery rule (see right) from the Scenery table must be used for this terrain feature.

Mystical: Roll a dice each time you allocate a wound or mortal wound to a model within 1" of any Mystical terrain features. On a 6+ the wound or mortal wound is negated.

KEYWORDS	SCENERY, NUMINOUS OCCULUM

OPHIDIAN ARCHWAY

The cyclopean stones and ancient carvings of an Ophidian Archway are home to
restless spirits and slumbering curses, which seep outward from the masonry to chill
the hearts of even the most resolute warriors.

DESCRIPTION

An Ophidian Archway is a single terrain
feature. It is an obstacle.

SCENERY RULES

Haunted: *A relic of the Age of Myth, an
Ophidian Archway is home to unquiet spirits
and slumbering magic.*

The Sinister scenery rule (see below) from
the Scenery table must be used for this
terrain feature.

Sinister: Subtract 1 from the Bravery
characteristic of units while they are within 1"
of any Sinister terrain features.

KEYWORDS	SCENERY, OPHIDIAN ARCHWAY

SHARDWRACK SPINES

Shardwrack Spines sprout from the ground like the teeth of some subterranean
predator. Attempts to clear them are often in vain, for even if their thick stems can be
hacked into, the severed stumps continue to grow and sharpen.

DESCRIPTION

A set of Shardwrack Spines is a terrain feature
that consists of 2-5 Shardwrack Spine models.
These must be set up as a single group,
with all models' bases touching at least one
other model's base from the group. A set of
Shardwrack Spines is an obstacle.

SCENERY RULES

Diamond-sharp Spikes: *Those seeking to make
their way past a cluster of Shardwrack Spines
must take great care, lest they tear themselves to
shreds upon their diamond-sharp spikes.*

The Deadly scenery rule (see right) from
the Scenery table must be used for this
terrain feature.

Deadly: Roll a dice for each unit that finishes
a normal move or charge move within 1" of
any Deadly terrain features. On a 1, that unit
suffers D3 mortal wounds.

KEYWORDS	SCENERY, SHARDWRACK SPINES

SIGMARITE MAUSOLEUM

The hallowed dead are housed in Sigmarite Mausoleums across the Mortal Realms.
But even these sanctified graves can be twisted by the fell magic of Nagash, and the
spirits within roused from their slumber.

DESCRIPTION

A Sigmarite Mausoleum is a terrain feature that consists of 3-6 Crypt models, 1-2 Statue models, 1-2 Gate models, and 7-14 Wall section models. These must be set up as a single group, with all models' bases touching at least two other models' bases from the group. A Sigmarite Mausoleum can be garrisoned.

GARRISON

The models making up the garrison of a Sigmarite Mausoleum must have a combined Wounds characteristic of 30 or less (if this would preclude all of the models in a unit from garrisoning the Sigmarite Mausoleum, then the unit cannot garrison the Sigmarite Mausoleum).

SCENERY RULES

Domain of the Dead: *A Sigmarite Mausoleum is a haunted and desolate place, cursed with a deathly energy that empowers the minions of Nagash.*

A Sigmarite Mausoleum is treated as a gravesite for the purposes of The Unquiet Dead battle trait from *Battletome: Legions of Nagash*. This is in addition to any gravesites that would normally be picked.

KEYWORDS	SCENERY, SIGMARITE MAUSOLEUM

WALLS AND FENCES

Where settlements arise, war is soon to follow. When marauding warbands and
rampaging armies march across the settled lands of the Mortal Realms, even
rudimentary defences can mean the difference between life and death.

DESCRIPTION

A set of Walls and Fences is a terrain feature that consists of 2-10 Wall and/or Fence models. These must be set up as a single group, with all models' bases touching at least one other model's base from the group. A set of Walls and Fences is an obstacle.

KEYWORDS	SCENERY, WALLS AND FENCES

● SCENERY WARSCROLL ●

WARSCRYER CITADEL

Each of these strongholds was hurled from Azyr upon a meteorite by Sigmar himself,
and now serve as potent sources of celestial magic – granting prophetic powers to
those who can master them.

DESCRIPTION
A Warscryer Citadel is a single terrain feature. It can be garrisoned. The apex of its main tower can be crowned either with crenellated battlements or a domed arcanoscope.

GARRISON
The models making up the garrison of a Warscryer Citadel must have a combined Wounds characteristic of 30 or less (if this would preclude all of the models in a unit from garrisoning the Warscryer Citadel, then the unit cannot garrison the Warscryer Citadel). In addition, a model with a Wounds characteristic of 10+ cannot garrison a Warscryer Citadel unless it has crenellated battlements (see right).

SCENERY RULES
Celestium Construct: *Within the glimmering stone of the citadel are rich veins of prophetic celestium. They provide guidance for those with the wisdom to divine them correctly.*

At the start of your hero phase, if any **HEROES** from your army are garrisoning this building, one of them can use the Azyrite realmstone bound within it to discern the skeins of future possibilities. If they do so, roll a dice. On a 2+ add 1 to the number of command points you receive that hero phase. On a 1 subtract 1 from the number of command points you receive that hero phase (to a minimum of 0).

Domed Arcanoscope: *By gazing long through the citadel's rune-etched arcanoscope, the scryer sees the passage of magical energy through the aether, and instinctively knows the disruptive counter-phrases and gestures that can disperse them before their effect takes hold.*

In the enemy hero phase, if any **HEROES** from your army are garrisoning a Warscryer Citadel with a domed arcanoscope, one of them can attempt to unbind one spell in the same manner as a **WIZARD**. If they can already unbind spells, they can attempt to unbind one additional spell.

Crenellated Battlements: *Certain Warscryer Citadels have towers that are capped with battlements, providing a formidable station from which infantry and even winged beasts can overlook the surrounding lands.*

If a Warscryer Citadel has crenellated battlements, it can be garrisoned by a single **MONSTER** that can fly, in addition to the other models that can garrison it.

| KEYWORDS | SCENERY, WARSCRYER CITADEL |

NEW SUMMONING RULES

With the new edition of Warhammer Age of Sigmar, the way units are summoned into battle has changed. This section details the changes to summoning rules – including battle traits, abilities and spells – that have been printed in our range of published battletomes and other books. For veteran players who are familiar with the reinforcement points used in the last edition of the *General's Handbook*, you will find that summoned units no longer cost reinforcement points – in fact, reinforcement points are no longer used in Pitched Battle games at all.

BATTLETOME: BLADES OF KHORNE (2017)

BATTLE TRAITS

Add the following battle trait to the Battle Traits section (pg 79):

Summon Daemons of Khorne: *As the blood of battle flows and the skulls of enemies are taken in tribute, the daemons of Khorne go forth into the Mortal Realms in a tide of slaughter, ferocity and seething rage.*

You can summon units of **KHORNE DAEMONS** to the battlefield by expending Blood Tithe points instead of choosing a reward from the Blood Tithe table.

If you have 2 or more Blood Tithe points at the end of your movement phase, you can summon one or more units from the list below onto the battlefield, and add them to your army. Each unit you summon costs a number of Blood Tithe points, as shown on the list, and you can only summon a unit if you have enough Blood Tithe points to pay its cost. If you summon any units in this manner, your Blood Tithe points total is reset to zero immediately after the last unit has been set up (you cannot save any Blood Tithe points you did not use).

Summoned units must be set up wholly within 12" of a friendly **KHORNE HERO** and more than 9" from any enemy units.

The following units can be summoned to your army:

BLADES OF KHORNE UNIT	COST
1 Wrath of Khorne Bloodthirster	8
1 Bloodthirster of Insensate Rage	8
1 Bloodthirster of Unfettered Fury	8
20 Bloodletters	7
15 Bloodletters	6
10 Flesh Hounds	6
3 Bloodcrushers	5
1 Skull Cannon	5
10 Bloodletters	4
1 Blood Throne	4
5 Flesh Hounds	3
1 Skullmaster, Herald of Khorne	3
5 Bloodletters	2
1 Bloodmaster, Herald of Khorne	2

BLOOD TITHE TABLE

Change the result of 8 on the Blood Tithe table (pg 79) as follows:

Blood Pact: Pick a **KHORNE DAEMON** unit from the summoning list below and add it to your army. Set up the unit anywhere on the battlefield that is more than 9" from any enemy units. It cannot move in the following movement phase.

KARANAK

On the Karanak warscroll (pg 130), change the wording of the 'Call of the Hunt' ability as follows:

Call of the Hunt: Once per game, if Karanak is within 8" of his quarry during the hero phase, you can summon a unit of 5 Flesh Hounds to the battlefield, and add it to your army. The summoned unit must be set up wholly within 8" of Karanak and more than 9" from any enemy units. The summoned unit cannot move in the following movement phase.

SPELLS

The following spells from this book are no longer used:

- Summon Bloodthirster of Fury (pg 127)
- Summon Bloodthirster of Rage (pg 128)
- Summon Bloodthirster of Wrath (pg 129)
- Summon Flesh Hounds (pg 130)
- Summon Skullmaster (pg 132)
- Summon Bloodmaster (pg 132)
- Summon Bloodletters (pg 133)
- Summon Bloodcrushers (pg 134)
- Summon Skull Cannon (pg 135)
- Summon Blood Throne (pg 136)

BATTLETOME: DISCIPLES OF TZEENTCH (2017)

BATTLE TRAITS

Add the following battle trait to the Battle Traits section (pg 74):

Summon Daemons of Tzeentch: *The machinations of Tzeentch are unimaginably complex. To challenge the fractal plans of the Architect of Fate is to stand before the folding of reality and face strange daemons born from chaotic sorcery itself.*

You can summon units of **Tzeentch Daemons** to the battlefield by expending Fate Points. You receive 1 Fate Point each time a casting roll is successful, and the spell is not unbound. Note that you receive Fate Points whenever a spell is cast, be it by friend or foe – Tzeentch cares not from whence the magic flows!

If you have 5 or more Fate Points at the end of your movement phase, you can summon one or more units from the list below onto the battlefield, and add them to your army. Each unit you summon costs a number of Fate Points, as shown on the list, and you can only summon a unit if you have enough Fate Points to pay its cost.

Summoned units must be set up wholly within 12" of a friendly **Tzeentch Hero** and more than 9" from any enemy units. Subtract the cost of the summoned unit from the number of Fate Points you have immediately after the summoned unit has been set up.

The following units can be summoned to your army:

DISCIPLES OF TZEENTCH UNIT	COST
1 Lord of Change	36
1 Herald of Tzeentch on Burning Chariot	24
10 Pink Horrors of Tzeentch	20
1 Burning Chariot of Tzeentch	18
3 Flamers of Tzeentch	18
1 Exalted Flamer of Tzeentch	12
1 Herald of Tzeentch	12
1 Herald of Tzeentch on Disc	12
10 Blue Horrors of Tzeentch	10
10 Brimstone Horrors of Tzeentch	10
3 Screamers of Tzeentch	10

BLUE HORRORS

On the Blue Horrors of Tzeentch warscroll (pg 123), change the wording of the 'Split' ability as follows:

Split: *When a Pink Horror is slain, its remains split into two smaller Blue Horrors, each grumbling and snarling in annoyance. These lesser forms may take petty vengeance on those responsible before scuttling off, or gather their fellow lesser daemons to renew the assault twice over.*

If a friendly **Pink Horror** model is slain, you can either take petty vengeance or receive 2 Blue Horror Points. If you take petty vengeance, pick an enemy unit within 9" of the slain **Pink Horror** and roll a dice. On a 6+ that enemy unit suffers 1 mortal wound. Any Blue Horror Points you receive can be used instead of or as well as Fate Points when you summon a **Blue Horrors** unit to the battlefield.

BRIMSTONE HORRORS

On the Brimstone Horrors of Tzeentch warscroll (pg 123), change the wording of the 'Split Again' ability as follows:

Split Again: *When a Blue Horror is slain they split into two Brimstone Horrors that burn with the need to wreak havoc. These lesser forms may take petty vengeance on those responsible before scuttling off, or gather their fellow lesser daemons to renew the assault twice over.*

If a friendly **Blue Horror** model is slain, you can either take petty vengeance or receive 1 Brimstone Horror Point. If you take petty vengeance, pick an enemy unit within 9" of the slain **Blue Horror** and roll a dice. On a 6+ that enemy unit suffers 1 mortal wound. Any Brimstone Horror Points you receive can be used instead of or as well as Fate Points when you summon a **Brimstone Horrors** unit to the battlefield.

SPELLS

The following spells from this book are no longer used:

- Summon Lord of Change (pg 114)
- Summon Burning Herald (pg 116)
- Summon Herald on Disc (pg 117)
- Summon Herald of Tzeentch (pg 118)
- Summon Screamers (pg 119)
- Summon Burning Chariot (pg 120)
- Summon Exalted Flamer (pg 121)
- Summon Flamers of Tzeentch (pg 121)
- Summon Pink Horrors (pg 122)

BATTLETOME: EVERCHOSEN (2015)

GAUNT SUMMONER OF TZEENTCH

On the Gaunt Summoner of Tzeentch warscroll (pg 101) change the 'Book of Profane Secrets' ability as follows:

Book of Profane Secrets:
Whispering fell incantations, a Gaunt Summoner can temporarily divert the path of a Realmgate, allowing malefic Chaos entities to manifest on the battlefield.

Once per battle, at the end of your movement phase, if this model is within 9" of a **Realmgate** it can use its Book of Profane Secrets. If it does so, you can summon 1 unit from the list below to the battlefield, and add it to your army. The summoned unit must be set up wholly within 9" of a this model and wholly within 9" of the **Realmgate**, and more than 9" from any enemy units.

Choose a unit from the following list:

- 10 Pink Horrors
- 10 Bloodletters
- 10 Plaguebearers
- 10 Daemonettes

GRAND ALLIANCE: CHAOS (2016)

GREAT BRAY-SHAMAN

On the Great Bray-Shaman warscroll (pg 197), replace the 'Savage Dominion' spell with the following:

Devolve: *The Bray-Shaman magnifies the savage and animalistic parts of the foe's psyche until they are no more than growling beasts.*

Devolve has a casting value of 7. If successfully cast, pick an enemy unit within 18" of the caster that is visible to them and not within 3" of any friendly units. Your opponent must move that unit 2D6 inches. In addition, that unit must finish that move as close as possible to the model from the caster's army that was nearest at the start of that move.

MUTALITH VORTEX BEAST

On the Mutalith Vortex Beast (and Mutalith Vortex Beast of Tzeentch) warscroll (pg 225), change the result of 6 on the 'Aura of Mutation' table as follows:

6. *Spawnchange:* The target unit suffers D6 mortal wounds. If at least one model is slain by these mortal wounds, set up a **Chaos Spawn** within 3" of the target unit and add it to your army.

LORD SKREECH VERMINKING

On the Lord Skreech Verminking warscroll (pg 241), change 'The Dreaded Thirteenth Spell' as follows:

The Dreaded Thirteenth Spell:
With a sickening lurch, the fabric of reality is torn open by the twisting, mutating power of the Great Horned Rat.

The Dreaded Thirteenth Spell has a casting value of 8. If successfully cast, pick an enemy unit within 13" of the caster that is visible to them and roll 13 dice. For each 4+ that unit suffers 1 mortal wound. If any models are slain by these mortal wounds, you can summon a unit of **Clanrats** to the battlefield, and add it to your army. The summoned unit has one model for each model slain by these mortal wounds. The summoned unit must be set up

wholly within 13" of Lord Skreech Verminking, and more than 9" from any enemy units. The summoned unit cannot move in the following movement phase.

SCREAMING BELL

On the Screaming Bell warscroll (pg 243), change the result of 12 on the 'Peal of Doom' table as follows:

A Stirring Beyond the Veil: You can summon a **Verminlord** to the battlefield and add it to your army. The summoned unit must be set up wholly within 24" of this model, and more than 9" from any enemy units. This result can be used once per battle. If you roll this result again, you must instead choose another result between 2 and 11.

SPELLS

The following spells from this book are no longer used:

- Summon Keeper of Secrets (pg 163)
- Summon Herald of Slaanesh (pg 165)
- Summon Seeker Herald (pg 166)
- Summon Hellflayer (pg 167)
- Summon Exalted Herald (pg 169)
- Summon Fiends of Slaanesh (pg 173)
- Summon Daemonettes (pg 175)
- Summon Seekers (pg 177)
- Summon Seeker Chariot (pg 179)
- Summon Exalted Chariot (pg 181)
- Summon Furies (pg 185)
- Summon Daemon Prince (pg 27, pg 187)
- Summon Soul Grinder (pg 189)
- Savage Dominion (pg 197)

BATTLETOME: SERAPHON (2015)

ENGINE OF THE GODS

On the Engine of the Gods warscroll (pg 133), change the result of 14-17 on the 'Cosmic Engine' table as follows:

You can summon a unit from the list below to the battlefield, and add it to your army. The summoned unit must be set up wholly within 12" of this model and more than 9" from any enemy units.

Choose a unit from the following list:

- 20 Skinks
- 10 Saurus Warriors
- 3 Ripperdactyls
- 3 Terradons

SPELLS

The following spells from this book are no longer used:

- Summon Oldblood (pg 102)
- Summon Sunblood (pg 103)
- Summon Saurus Warlord (pg 105)
- Summon Eternity Warden (pg 106)
- Summon Saurus Guard (pg 107)
- Summon Carnosaur (pg 109)
- Summon Knight Veteran (pg 110)
- Summon Saurus (p111)
- Summon Astrolith Bearer (pg 112)
- Summon Saurus Knights (pg 113)
- Summon Starseer (pg 114)
- Summon Starpriest (pg 115)
- Summon Troglodon (pg 117)
- Summon Skink Priest (pg 118)
- Summon Skinks (pg 119)
- Summon Chameleon Skinks (pg 120)
- Summon Salamanders (pg 121)
- Summon Razordons (pg 122)
- Summon Skink Handlers (pg 123)
- Summon Kroxigor (pg 124)
- Summon Bastiladon (pg 125)
- Summon Terradons (pg 127)
- Summon Ripperdactyls (pg 129)
- Summon Stegadon (pg 131)
- Summon Engine of the Gods (pg 133)

BATTLETOME: SYLVANETH (2016)

ALARIELLE THE EVERQUEEN

On the Alarielle the Everqueen warscroll (pg 132), change the 'Soul Amphorae' ability as follows:

Soul Amphorae: *With a gesture, Alarielle can summon forth healing pollens and soul seeds from the amphorae arrayed around her mount.*

In your hero phase, you can heal D3 wounds allocated to each SYLVANETH model within 30" of this model. Once per battle, in your hero phase, instead of using this ability to heal, you can summon 1 unit from the list below to the battlefield, and add it to your army. The summoned unit must be set up wholly within 9" of this model and more than 9" from any enemy units. That unit cannot move in the following movement phase.

Choose a unit from the following list:

- 20 Dryads
- 10 Tree-Revenants
- 10 Spite-Revenants
- 3 Kurnoth Hunters
- 1 Branchwych
- 1 Treelord

BRANCHWRAITH

On the Branchwraith warscroll (pg 137), change the 'Roused to Wrath' spell as follows:

Roused to Wrath: *With biting verses, the Branchwraith sings to its allies through the realmroots, calling them forth to join the reaping.*

Roused to Wrath has a casting value of 7. If successfully cast, you can summon a unit of 10 DRYADS and add it to your army. The summoned unit must be set up more than 9" from any enemy units, and wholly on or within a SYLVANETH WYLDWOOD that is within 12" of the caster. The summoned unit cannot move in the following movement phase.

ALLEGIANCE ABILITIES

In this section you will find allegiance abilities for a number of factions that represent the different ways the varied armies of the Mortal Realms go to war. Rules for using allegiance abilities can be found in the core rules.

DARKLING COVENS

This section describes the allegiance abilities available to a Darkling Covens army, including battle traits for the army, command traits for its general and the artefacts of power available to its heroes.

BATTLE TRAITS

Lethal Coordination: *Dreadspears, Bleakswords and Darkshards are mercilessly trained to work in close cooperation, each one supporting the other upon the battlefield. They use this hard-earned expertise to field formations that have Bleakswords in the front rank, Dreadspears just behind them, and Darkshards at the rear.*

The **DREADSPEARS**' Formidable Bastion ability, the **BLEAKSWORDS**' Quicksilver Strike ability, and the **DARKSHARDS**' Storm of Iron-tipped Bolts ability are each based upon the number of models in the unit. When working out the number of models in a unit when one of these units uses one of these abilities, add the number of friendly **DREADSPEARS**, **BLEAKSWORDS** and **DARKSHARDS** models from other units that are within 6" of it.

For example, if a unit of 10 **DARKSHARDS** is within 6" of 10 friendly **DREADSPEAR** models when it attacks in the shooting phase, then it would count as having 20 models for the purposes of its Storm of Iron-tipped Bolts ability.

Tyrannical Ruler: *The leader of a Darkling Coven rules through bloodshed and intimidation; they believe that respect counts for nothing unless it is backed by fear.*

If a friendly **DARKLING COVEN** unit has to take a battleshock test when they are within 3" of the general, you can choose to inflict a mortal wound on the unit instead of taking the battleshock test.

If the general of your army is a **DARKLING COVEN** model you can use the following command abilities:

Command Underlings: You can use this command ability in your hero phase. If you do so, pick a friendly **DARKLING COVEN** unit wholly within 12" of your general. Until your next hero phase, that unit can run and still shoot and/or charge in the same turn.

Inspire Hatred: You can use this command ability at the start of the combat phase. If you do so, pick a friendly **DARKLING COVEN** unit wholly within 12" of your general. You can re-roll wound rolls of 1 for attacks made by that unit in that combat phase.

COMMAND TRAITS

D6   Command Trait

1   Merciless: *Tales of this cruel despot's treatment of those that fall into their clutches fill the enemy with dread.*

D3 additional models flee from enemy units that fail a battleshock test within 12" of this general.

2   Arrogant Prowess: *This supreme battle-master despatches any foe with spiteful indifference.*

You can re-roll hit rolls of 1 for this general.

3   Sustained by Misery: *Death, pain and suffering are food and drink to this depraved megalomaniac.*

At the end of the combat phase, if at least one enemy model was slain within 12" of this general during that combat phase, you can heal D3 wounds that have been allocated to this general.

4   Master of the Sorcerous Arts: *This leader has mastered the magical arts.*

If this general is a **WIZARD**, add 1 to casting and unbinding rolls for them. If this general is not a **WIZARD**, they gain the **WIZARD** keyword and can cast and unbind spells in the same manner as a **SORCERESS** from the Sorceress warscroll.

5   Effortless Grace: *This arrogant warrior easily parries his opponent's clumsy attacks.*

Add 1 to save rolls for this general.

6   Impossibly Swift: *This dark warrior moves with superhuman swiftness, making them an incredibly difficult target.*

Subtract 1 from hit rolls for attacks that target this general.

ARTEFACTS OF POWER

D6   Artefact

1   Shadowshroud Ring: *If this obsidian ring is turned round the wearer's finger three times, it emits a cloud of black shadow that engulfs the ring-bearer.*

Once per battle, in your hero phase, the bearer can use this artefact. If they do so, visibility to and from the bearer is limited to a maximum distance of 3" until your next hero phase. In addition, the bearer can fly until your next hero phase.

2   Incorporeal Retainer: *In addition to armies of bewitched warriors protecting her, a Sorceress may employ a creature of pure shadow to deflect the strikes of her enemies.*

Roll a dice each time the bearer suffers a wound or mortal wound. On a 6+, the wound is negated.

3   Anklet of Epiphany: *This cuff tethers its wearer to the realm in which they stand, allowing them to draw upon buried energies that have lain fallow since the Age of Myth.*

Add 6" to the range of any spells successfully cast by the bearer while they are within 1" of a terrain feature.

4   Decanter of Egos: *When released, the restless animus stored within this flask drives nearby warriors to move swiftly across the battlefield.*

Once per battle, at the start of your movement phase, the bearer can use this artefact. If they do so, for that movement phase add 3" to the Move characteristic of friendly **DARKLING COVEN** units that are wholly within 12" of the bearer at the start of the phase.

5   Heart of Woe: *Over time, this amulet becomes infused with the life-force of its wearer. Should they fall in battle, the blackened gem ruptures in an explosion of spiteful energy.*

If the bearer is slain, before they are removed from play each enemy unit within 3" of the bearer suffers D3 mortal wounds.

6   Shadesliver: *This thin-bladed dagger becomes deadlier each time it is bathed in the blood of its victims.*

Pick one of the bearer's melee weapons. If that weapon inflicts any wounds in the combat phase, add 1 to its Damage characteristic for the rest of the battle, starting from the next combat phase in which it is used. This effect is cumulative.

ALLEGIANCE ABILITIES
DISPOSSESSED

This section describes the allegiance abilities available to a Dispossessed army, including battle traits for the army, command traits for its general and the artefacts of power available to its heroes.

BATTLE TRAITS

Stubborn to the End: *The Dispossessed are renowned for their refusal to admit defeat, especially in the face of overwhelming odds.*

If you roll a 1, 2 or 3 (before modifiers are applied) when taking a battleshock test for a friendly **DISPOSSESSED** unit, that unit is treated as having passed the battleshock test irrespective of any modifiers to the battleshock test or their Bravery characteristic.

Grudgebound: *When a Dispossessed army goes to war, sparks of bitterness over ancient grudges are fanned into seething flames.*

After set-up is complete, but before the battle begins, choose or roll for a grudge from the table on the right. The rules for that grudge apply to all friendly **DISPOSSESSED** units for the duration of the battle.

GRUDGES

D6	Grudge
1	**Stuck-up:** You can re-roll hit rolls of 1 for friendly **DISPOSSESSED** units if the target of the attack is an enemy **HERO**.
2	**Speed Merchants:** You can re-roll hit rolls of 1 for friendly **DISPOSSESSED** units if the target of the attack has a Move characteristic of 10+.
3	**Monstrous Cheaters:** You can re-roll hit rolls of 1 for friendly **DISPOSSESSED** units if the target of the attack is an enemy **MONSTER**.
4	**Cowardly Hordes:** You can re-roll hit rolls of 1 for friendly **DISPOSSESSED** units if the target of the attack is in an enemy unit that had twenty or more models when it was set up.
5	**Shoddy Craftsmanship:** You can re-roll hit rolls of 1 for friendly **DISPOSSESSED** units if the target of the attack has a Save characteristic of 2+, 3+, or 4+ .
6	**Sneaky Ambushers:** You can re-roll hit rolls of 1 for friendly **DISPOSSESSED** units if the target of the attack is in cover, or did not start the battle set up on the battlefield.

COMMAND TRAITS

D6	Command Trait
1	**Resolute:** *This general inspires his warriors to new heights of stubbornness.* Friendly **DISPOSSESSED** units wholly within 12" of this general pass battleshock tests on a roll of 1 to 4, rather than only on a roll of 1 to 3 (see the Stubborn to the End battle trait).
2	**Resilient:** *This general is hale and hearty, even by the doughty standards of the Dispossessed.* Add 1 to this general's Wounds characteristic.
3	**Siegemaster:** *Neither brick nor stone can stand in the path of this duardin's rage.* Do not add 1 to the save rolls of enemy units that are in cover if they are attacked by this general or a friendly **DISPOSSESSED** unit wholly within 12" of this general.
4	**Unforgiving:** *Those who strike this duardin are soon repaid with his untempered wrath.* Add 1 to wound rolls for attacks made by this general if the target is from a unit that has inflicted any wounds on this general.
5	**Battle Fury:** *In the midst of combat this mighty warrior is known to fly into a whirl of violence.* Roll a dice after this general completes their attacks in the combat phase; on a roll of 6+ they can fight again (do not roll again after completing the second set of attacks).
6	**Grudgebearer:** *This duardin is quick to add new names to his list of grudges.* Once per battle, if your general has not been slain, you can pick a new grudge in your hero phase to replace the original grudge you chose for your army (see battle traits).

ARTEFACTS OF POWER

D6 Artefact

1 Heavy Metal Ingot: *Imbued with the eternal might of mountains, the Ingot makes an immovable object and an unstoppable force of the duardin who carries it.*

You can re-roll failed save rolls for the bearer as long as they have not made a move in the same turn.

2 Ancestral Pickaxe: *The duardin of old carved mighty tunnels underneath the lands of the Mortal Realms. This axe is one of the few tools to have survived from that bygone age.*

Once per the battle, at the start of your movement phase, you can remove the bearer and up to 1 other friendly **Dispossessed** unit within 3" of the bearer from the battlefield. Set them up again at the end of your next movement phase, anywhere on the battlefield, wholly within 6" of each other and more than 9" away from enemy models.

3 Teardrop of Grungni: *When this unembellished orb is hurled at the foe it releases a searing spray of molten lead. Those not slain outright are encased in the rapidly cooling metal.*

Once per battle, at the start of your shooting phase, pick an enemy unit within 6" of the bearer. That unit suffers D3 mortal wounds. In addition, if the target is a **Hero** or **Monster**, it must halve its Move characteristic in its next movement phase.

4 Grudge Rune: *Etched on this symbol of power is the name of one who has stoked the ire of this duardin hero. When the grudge is fulfilled, the name fades so that a new name can be carved.*

After set up is complete but before the battle begins, pick an enemy **Hero**. You can re-roll failed hit and wound rolls for the bearer if the target of the attack is the enemy **Hero** you picked.

5 Piledriver Gauntlets: *Created by Avrik Fortbuilder to lay foundation stones in the most unyielding surfaces across the realms, these master-crafted gloves are equally useful for knocking the enemy off their feet.*

At the start of the combat phase, you can declare that the bearer will strike the ground instead of attacking. If you do so, in that combat phase, subtract 1 from hit rolls for attacks made by enemy models that are within 6" of the bearer when they attack.

6 Resounding Gromrilhorn: *Like the metal from which it is forged, this horn's blast is pure and true, and it fills every duardin heart with unwavering vigour.*

Once per battle, at the start of your hero phase, the bearer can use this artefact. If they do so, add 2 to the Bravery characteristic of friendly **Dispossessed** units until your next hero phase.

ALLEGIANCE ABILITIES
FREE PEOPLES

This section describes the allegiance abilities available to a Free Peoples army, including battle traits for the army, command traits for its general and the artefacts of power available to its heroes.

BATTLE TRAITS

Defiant Avengers: *The forces of Order are confident of their abilities and are determined to drive the minions of Chaos from the Mortal Realms.*

You can re-roll battleshock tests for friendly **FREE PEOPLES** units.

Freeguild Great Companies: *The backbone of the Free Peoples' diverse army is its regiments of well-drilled infantry – serried ranks of troops that support each other against the foe.*

You can organise friendly **FREE PEOPLES** units into Freeguild Great Companies before set-up begins. You must tell your opponent which of your units are in each Freeguild Great Company that you form.

When you form a Freeguild Great Company before the battle, it must consist of one **FREEGUILD GUARD** unit with at least 20 models, and two other **FREEGUILD** units of any type (including other **FREEGUILD GUARD** units) that have at least 10 models each.

For example, a Great Company might have one unit of 30 **FREEGUILD GUARD**, one unit of 15 **FREEGUILD CROSSBOWMEN**, and one unit of 10 **FREEGUILD GREATSWORDS**.

At the end of each enemy charge phase, units in a Freeguild Great Company can lend support to other units from their Great Company if all of the following conditions apply:

- The unit lending support is more than 3" from the enemy.

- The unit being supported is within 3" of the enemy.

- The two units are wholly within 12" of each other.

A unit lending support to another unit from its Great Company can either shoot as if it were your shooting phase, or charge as if it were your charge phase.

COMMAND TRAITS

D6	Command Trait
1	**Inspiring:** *The mere sight of this general on the battlefield imbues his warriors with unflagging courage.* Friendly **FREE PEOPLES** units wholly within 12" of this general do not have to take battleshock tests.
2	**Battle-tested Veteran:** *Through countless battles, this general has learnt to continually advance and adapt their strategies.* At the start of your hero phase, if this general is on the battlefield roll a dice. On a 5+ you receive 1 extra command point.
3	**Shrewd Commander:** *Even before setting foot upon the battlefield, this general has leveraged every advantage to ensure victory.* Roll on the Triumph table at the start of the battle. This is in addition to the roll for winning a **major victory** in your last battle.
4	**Indomitable:** *This general expertly puts into practice the art of defensive warfare.* Add 1 to save rolls for friendly **FREE PEOPLES** units if they are wholly within 12" of this general and have not made a charge move in the same turn.
5	**Righteous Fury:** *This warrior despises the servants of the Dark Gods more so than any other enemy, and will execute them without mercy wherever they are found.* Add 1 to wound rolls for attacks made by this general if the target of the attack has the **CHAOS** keyword.
6	**Grim Resolve:** *Having survived many blows that would kill most mortals, this general has developed a dour and dauntless aspect.* Add 1 to this general's Wounds characteristic.

ARTEFACTS OF POWER

D6 **Artefact**

1 **Armour of Meteoric Iron:** *Forged from the metal of a fallen star, it is said that no mortal blade can pierce the Armour of Meteoric Iron.*

Add 1 to save rolls for the bearer.

2 **Blade of the Realms:** *Magically attuned to each of the Eight Realms, the Blade of the Realms can slip in and out of reality at a thought. When wielded by a true warrior, no mortal armour can stop it.*

Pick one of the bearer's melee weapons. Each time you make a wound roll of 6+ for that weapon, the target suffers 1 mortal wound in addition to any other damage the attack inflicts.

3 **Luckstone:** *It is said this rune-etched pebble attracts good fortune like a magnet, and that it has survived not just the destruction of the World Before Time, but a dozen worlds before it.*

You can re-roll one failed hit, wound or save roll for the bearer each turn.

4 **The Broken Shackle:** *A symbol of the Free Peoples' courage and heritage, this sundered pair of manacles allows the wearer to stride unimpeded through even the thickest combats.*

The bearer can retreat and charge as if it can fly. In addition, the bearer can retreat and charge in the same turn.

5 **Writ of Dominion:** *A record of the Free Peoples' decree to take back what is theirs, the words on this magically imbued scroll fill all who hear them with grim determination.*

Once per battle, at the start of your hero phase, the bearer can use this artefact. If they do so, the bearer cannot move until your next hero phase. However, until your next hero phase, add 1 to wound rolls for attacks made by friendly **FREE PEOPLES** units that are wholly within 12" of the bearer.

6 **Flag of the Conquerors:** *Wherever this flag is planted the Free Peoples make their stand.*

Add 1 to the Bravery characteristic of friendly **FREE PEOPLES** units that are wholly within 12" of the bearer. In addition, add 1 to charge rolls for friendly **FREE PEOPLES** units that are wholly within 12" of the bearer when the charge roll is made.

ALLEGIANCE ABILITIES
FYRESLAYERS

This section describes the allegiance abilities available to a Fyreslayers army, including battle traits for the army, command traits for its general and the artefacts of power available to its heroes.

BATTLE TRAITS

Ur-gold Runes: *Ur-gold is a source of strength for the Fyreslayers. In battle a warrior's runes are awakened, filling them with the blazing power of Grimnir.*

At the start of your hero phase, you can activate one of the following six ur-gold runes. State which rune will be activated and roll a dice. On a 1-5, the rune has the standard effect. On a 6+ it also has the enhanced effect. The effect(s) of the rune lasts until the start of your next hero phase.

The power of each ur-gold rune can only be activated once in each battle, and no more than one can be activated at the same time. Once you have used a rune, you can choose a new one to use in your next hero phase, but you cannot use the same one again.

Rune of Fury: You can re-roll hit rolls of 1 in the combat phase for attacks made by friendly **FYRESLAYER** units.
Enhanced Effect: Add 1 to the Attacks characteristic of melee weapons used by friendly **FYRESLAYER** units.

Rune of Searing Heat: Add 1 to the Damage characteristic of melee and missile weapons used by friendly **FYRESLAYER** units if the wound roll for the attack was 6+.
Enhanced Effect: Enemy units within 3" of any friendly **FYRESLAYERS** when this rune is activated in the hero phase suffer 1 mortal wound.

Rune of Awakened Steel: Improve the Rend characteristic of melee weapons used by friendly **FYRESLAYER** units by 1.
Enhanced Effect: Improve the Rend characteristic by a further 1.

Rune of Fiery Determination: Friendly **FYRESLAYER** units do not have to take battleshock tests.
Enhanced Effect: Friendly **FYRESLAYER** models that are slain in the combat phase are not removed until the end of the phase, and in the meantime can still fight normally.

Rune of Relentless Zeal: Add 4" to the Move characteristic of friendly **FYRESLAYER** units.
Enhanced Effect: Add 4 to charge rolls for friendly **FYRESLAYER** units.

Rune of Farsight: Add 8" to the Range characteristic of Fyresteel Throwing Axes used by friendly **FYRESLAYER** units.
Enhanced Effect: Re-roll hit rolls of 1 for attacks made with Fyresteel Throwing Axes by friendly **FYRESLAYER** units.

COMMAND TRAITS

D6	Command Trait
1	**Fury of the Fyreslayers:** *This general drives his warriors to fall upon the enemy with the wrath of a raging volcano.* Friendly **FYRESLAYER** units that start a combat phase wholly within 12" of this general can move an additional 3" when they pile in.
2	**Exemplar of the Ancestor:** *In battle, this general embodies the bravery of his ancestors, inspiring those Fyreslayers fighting alongside him to greater acts of courage.* Friendly **FYRESLAYER** units wholly within 12" of this general do not have to take battleshock tests.
3	**Blood of the Berserker:** *In the thick of combat, this warrior allows their battle-lust to take over, transforming them into a whirling storm of implacable fury.* Once per battle, this general can fight again immediately after they have fought.
4	**Iron of the Guardian:** *The runes hammered into this Fyreslayer's flesh allow him to shrug off all but the most devastating blows.* Worsen the Rend characteristic of enemy weapons by 1, to a minimum of '-', if they target this general.
5	**Destroyer of Foes:** *With a mighty smite, this general can fell a rampaging daemon or bring low a towering gargant.* Add 1 to the Damage characteristic of melee and missile weapons used by this general if the wound roll for the attack is 6+.
6	**Spirit of Grimnir:** *The runes of this blessed champion are touched by the power of the mighty warrior-god.* Once per battle, as long as this general has not been slain, you can use a dice roll of 5+ to activate an ur-gold rune's enhanced effect instead of a dice roll of 6+ (see battle traits).

ARTEFACTS OF POWER

D6   Artefact

1   Igneous Plate: *The Igneous Plate retains the fires of its forging. Though blistering to the touch and hence very painful to wear, the Igneous Plate melts the blades of those that strike it.*

Subtract 1 from hit rolls for melee weapons that target the bearer if neither the attacker nor the bearer charged during this turn.

2   Ancestor Rune: *With this rune many great wyrms of the Age of Myth were slain.*

Pick one of the bearer's melee weapons. Add 1 to wound rolls for that weapon if the target is a **Monster**.

3   Obsidian Coronet: *Carved from pure volcanic glass, this lustrous helm absorbs the burning glow of nearby runes and projects their power across the battlefield.*

Add 6" to the range of command abilities if the bearer is chosen as the model from which the range of a command ability is measured.

4   Volcanic Rune: *The blood of those slain by a weapon bearing this rune is instantly transmuted so that it erupts with the burning fury of a Magmadroth.*

At the end of the combat phase, roll a dice for each enemy unit within 1" of the bearer. On a 3+ that unit suffers 1 mortal wound.

5   Ash-plume Sigil: *By chanting the name of this rune, its bearer can call down a column of choking soot that clogs the flow of foul magic.*

Once per battle, in your hero phase, you can automatically dispel one predatory endless spell within 15" of the bearer.

6   Meteoric Axe: *Said to have been forged by Ignoset, the living volcano, this blade is hurled skyward, and from the clouds it descends upon its enemies with the force of a falling star.*

Increase the Range characteristic of the bearer's Fyresteel Throwing Axe to 16", and the Damage characteristic to D3.

WARSCROLL BATTALION
VOSTARG LODGE

Beneath the smouldering volcanoes of the Cynder Peaks, the hammers of the Vostarg lodge ring ceaselessly upon their anvils like drums of war. Among the oldest of the Aqshy Fyreslayer lodges, the Vostarg can trace their lineage back to the legendary Vosforge, and they are the only scions of the original Vostarg lodge still to bear that name. From their sprawling magmahold of Furios Peak, the might of the Vostarg casts a blazing glow across the lands, and their reputation as brutal mercenaries and fearsome warriors stretches far beyond the borders of their domain.

ORGANISATION

A Vostarg Lodge consists of the following warscroll battalions:

- 1 Lords of the Lodge (must contain 1 additional unit of Hearthguard Berzerkers)

- 1 Warrior Kinband

A Vostarg Lodge may also contain:

- 0-2 warscroll battalions chosen in any combination from the following list:

  - Warrior Kinband

  - Forge Brethren

- Any number of additional **FYRESLAYER** units

If a Vostarg Lodge contains the maximum number of battalions, it gains the Dour and Fearless ability from the Grand Fyrd warscroll battalion in *Battletome: Fyreslayers*.

ABILITIES

Proud Lineage: *The Fyreslayers of the Vostarg lodge fight to the very end, slaying enemies in the name of their ancestors even as they themselves face death.*

If the Rune of Fiery Determination (pg 108) is activated, it always has its enhanced effect on units from a Vostarg Lodge.

Fearsome Reputation: *The fury of the Vostarg lodge is known throughout Aqshy and beyond, causing even the most battle-hardened enemies to tremble at their approach.*

Subtract 1 from the Bravery characteristic of enemy units while they are within 3" of any units from a Vostarg Lodge.

WARSCROLL BATTALION
GREYFYRD LODGE

Mercenary wanderers, the Greyfyrd lodge travel the realms in search of precious ur-gold to smelt within their forges. From the heart of their great magmahold Gateswold, where portals to many realms lurk beneath megalithic obstinite mountains, the Greyfyrds embark on crusades into the far reaches of the Mortal Realms. In many realms the lodge are much sought-after as mercenaries, and their warriors have changed the fates of the Ninefold Kingdoms of Obsidia, the Gloom tribes of Shyish and the Neolantic Bloodlands among uncounted others.

ORGANISATION

A Greyfyrd Lodge consists of the following warscroll battalions:

- 1 Lords of the Lodge

- 1 Warrior Kinband (must contain 1 additional unit of Vulkite Berzerkers)

A Greyfyrd Lodge may also contain:

- 0-2 warscroll battalions chosen in any combination from the following list:

  - Warrior Kinband

  - Forge Brethren

- Any number of additional **Fyreslayer** units

If a Greyfyrd Lodge contains the maximum number of battalions, it gains the Dour and Fearless ability from the Grand Fyrd warscroll battalion in *Battletome: Fyreslayers*.

ABILITIES

Mercenary Wanderers: *The warriors of the Greyfyrd lodge have travelled the realms, and have perfected the savage art of ambushing their enemies.*

Instead of setting up a unit from a Greyfyrd Lodge on the battlefield, you can place it to one side and say that it is using the obstinite mountain portals. If you do, you can roll a D3 for the unit at the end of any of your movement phases and look up the result on the table below.

D3	Result
1	**Difficult Journey:** The unit is still travelling to the battlefield; it does not arrive in this turn but you can roll for it again in your next turn.
2	**Flank March:** Set up the unit wholly within 6" of the edge of the battlefield, not in enemy territory and more than 9" from any enemy units.
3	**Rear March:** Set up the unit wholly within 6" of the edge of the battlefield, anywhere in enemy territory and more than 9" from any enemy units.

ALLEGIANCE ABILITIES
SERAPHON

This section describes the allegiance abilities available to a Seraphon army, including battle traits for the army, command traits for its general and the artefacts of power available to its heroes.

BATTLE TRAITS

Masters of Order: *The ancient slann are amongst the greatest wizards in existence, and they shape the very stars with their magic.*

SLANN WIZARDS can attempt to unbind enemy spells that are cast anywhere on the battlefield, rather than only those cast within 30". In addition, if the casting roll for a **SLANN WIZARD** is a 10+, and the spell is successfully cast, you can add 6" to the range of the spell.

Lords of Space and Time: *The slann are able to bridge any distance in an instant, as mortal concerns such as space and time hold little meaning for them.*

In your hero phase, you can pick a friendly **SERAPHON** unit anywhere on the battlefield to be transported through space and time. If you do so, roll a dice for the unit and look up the result on the table on the right.

D6	Effect
1-2	**Contemplating the Cosmos:** The unit cannot move or charge this turn.
3-4	**Spatial Displacement:** Remove the unit from the battlefield, and then set it back up anywhere that is more than 9" from an enemy unit. This counts as the unit's move for the next movement phase.
5-6	**Temporal Displacement:** As Spatial Displacement, except that the unit is also allowed to move in the next movement phase as normal.

Celestial Conjuration: *Channelling the power of Azyrite magic, the great Starmasters call upon the echoes of a bygone age to summon forth an army of Seraphon. These legendary warrior creatures are given corporeal form, the better to bring their wrath upon the forces of Chaos.*

You can summon units of **Seraphon** to the battlefield if you collect enough Celestial Conjuration Points. In your hero phase, before attempting to cast a spell with a **Slann** general, you can say that it will carry out Celestial Conjuration instead. If you do so, you receive 3 Celestial Conjuration points instead of being able to attempt to cast that spell. In addition, at the end of your hero phase you receive 1 Celestial Conjuration point if your general is a **Slann** and is on the battlefield, and D3 Celestial Conjuration points if there are one or more friendly **Saurus Astrolith Bearers** on the battlefield.

If you have 6 or more Celestial Conjuration points at the end of your movement phase, you can summon one or more units from the list on the right onto the battlefield, and add them to your army. Each unit you summon costs a number of Celestial Conjuration points, as shown on the list, and you can only summon a unit if you have enough Celestial Conjuration points to pay its cost.

Summoned units must be set up wholly within 12" of a friendly **Slann** or a friendly **Saurus Astrolith Bearer**, and more than 9" from any enemy units. Subtract the cost of the summoned unit from the number of Conjuration Points you have immediately after the summoned unit has been set up.

SERAPHON UNIT	COST
1 Bastiladon	24
1 Saurus Old Blood On Carnosaur	24
1 Saurus Scar-Veteran on Carnosaur	24
1 Stegadon	24
1 Engine of the Gods	18
3 Kroxigor	18
1 Saurus Astrolith Bearer	18
20 Saurus Warriors	18
1 Skink Starseer	18
1 Troglodon	18
5 Chameleon Skinks	12
3 Ripperdactyls	12
1 Saurus Eternity Warden	12
5 Saurus Guard	12
5 Saurus Knights	12
1 Saurus Oldblood	12
1 Saurus Scar-Veteran on Cold One	12
1 Saurus Sunblood	12
10 Saurus Warriors	12
1 Skink Priest	12
1 Skink Starpriest	12
3 Terradon Riders	12
3 Skink Handlers	6
10 Skinks	6
1 Razordon	6
1 Salamander	6

COMMAND TRAITS

Use the command traits table that corresponds to your general's keyword – **Slann**, **Saurus** or **Skink**. If your general has none of these keywords, it cannot have a Seraphon command trait.

D3 Slann Command Trait

1 **Arcane Might:** *With the authority of aeons, this powerful slann commands the flow of magic on the battlefield.*

You can re-roll one casting or unbinding roll for this general each hero phase.

2 **Vast Intellect:** *No secret is unknown to the mind of this unfathomable being.*

This general can use the Curse of Fates and Summon Starlight spells from the Skink Starseer and Skink Starpriest warscrolls.

3 **Great Rememberer:** *The manoeuvres ordered by this general are redolent of the countless constellations in the sky.*

If this general is on the battlefield, you can use the Lords of Space and Time battle trait twice in each of your hero phases rather than only once.

D3 Saurus Command Trait

1 **Disciplined Fury:** *When this saurus strikes, they do so with cold-blooded precision.*

You can re-roll hit rolls of 1 for attacks made with this general's melee weapons.

2 **Thickly Scaled Hide:** *The plated scales covering this general can deflect even the sharpest of blades.*

You can re-roll save rolls of 1 for this general.

3 **Mighty War Leader:** *This apex creature guides its warriors in battle with bellowing roars.*

At the start of your hero phase, if this general is on the battlefield, roll a dice. On a 5+ you receive 1 extra command point.

D3 Skink Command Trait

1 **Master of Star Rituals:** *The lights of Azyr shine brightly on this general.*

If this general is a **Skink Priest** from the Skink Priest warscroll, they can use the Celestial Rites ability from their warscroll twice in each of their hero phases rather than once. If they are not a **Skink Priest** from the Skink Priest warscroll, then they can use the Celestial Rites ability.

2 **Nimble:** *This skink is preternaturally agile.*

Add 1 to this general's Move characteristic. In addition, add 1 to save rolls for this general as long as they are not riding upon a mount.

3 **Cunning:** *With reptilian calculation this general looks for an opportunity to strike.*

Roll a dice at the start of the combat phase if this general is within 3" of an enemy **Hero**. On a 4+ the enemy **Hero** suffers 1 mortal wound.

ARTEFACTS OF POWER

D6 Artefact

1 Zoetic Dial: *As the constellations align with the facets of this mighty Astrolith, the strands of fate inexorably envelope its bearer.*

Roll a dice after set-up is complete, but before the battle begins. In the battle round corresponding to the number you roll, you can re-roll failed save rolls for the bearer. If you roll a 6, you can decide to use this ability at the start of any one battle round, rather than having to use it in the 6th battle round.

2 Incandescent Rectrices: *The light of a thousand stars shimmers along the length of this vibrant plumage, instilling the bearer with the restorative power of the heavens.*

Roll a dice the first time a wound is allocated to the bearer that would slay them. On a 1-2 the bearer is slain. On a 3+ heal D6 wounds allocated to the bearer instead.

3 Blade of Realities: *This weapon has existed in one form or another across every realm and in every reality. It is remembered into existence by the Starmasters to bring about the end of tyrants.*

Pick one of the bearer's melee weapons. Improve the Rend characteristic of that weapon by 1.

4 Light of Dracothion: *Gathered by the slann on their journey to Azyr, the light from the Great Drake's tears can wash away the foulest and most corruptive of energies.*

Once per battle, you can automatically unbind one spell cast by an enemy **WIZARD** within 15" of the bearer.

5 Coronal Shield: *Those who stand before the carrier of the Coronal Shield are blinded by the focused light of suns before they are immolated.*

At the start of each combat phase, roll a dice for each enemy unit within 3" of the bearer. On a 4+ subtract 1 from hit rolls for that unit in that combat phase.

6 Prism of Amyntok: *When angled correctly, the Prism of Amyntok can channel aetheric power from the skies of the Luminous Realm, blasting the bearer's foes with a beam of pure white energy.*

Once per the battle, at the start of your movement phase, pick an enemy unit within 12" of the bearer and roll a dice. On a 1 that unit suffers 1 mortal wound. On a 2-5 that unit suffers D3 mortal wounds. On a 6 that unit suffers D6 mortal wounds.

WARSCROLL BATTALION
FANGS OF SOTEK

The curving fangs of the constellation of Sotek rise above the Mortal Realms on nights when the winds of Azyr blow their strongest. Each shimmering star in this radiant formation is a Seraphon cohort waiting for the call of the slann Starmaster Zectoka. Blazing upon the tip of the longest tooth is Ku-Quar – when Zectoka summons the constellation to battle this saurus is often the first to step into the Mortal Realms. From the back of his bellowing Carnosaur, Ku-Quar leads a host of warriors and lumbering reptilian beasts into battle against the armies of Chaos.

ORGANISATION

A Fangs of Sotek battalion consists of the following:

- 1 Slann Starmaster (Zectoka)

- 1 Saurus Oldblood on Carnosaur (Ku-Quar)

- 1 Sunclaw Starhost battalion

A Fangs of Sotek battalion may also contain:

- 0-4 warscroll battalions chosen in any combination from the following list:

  - Sunclaw Starhost

  - Firelance Starhost

  - Eternal Starhost

  - Thunderquake Starhost

- Any number of additional **SERAPHON** units

If a Fangs of Sotek battalion contains the maximum number of battalions, it gains the Strategic Mastery ability from the Starbeast Constellation warscroll battalion in *Battletome: Seraphon*.

ABILITIES

First to Battle: *Like the tip of a spear or head of an arrow, the Fangs of Sotek drive forward with blinding speed to strike at the enemy.*

In the first battle round, add 3" to the Move characteristic of Fangs of Sotek units, excluding Zectoka.

First Oldblood: *The ancient saurus Ku-Quar has seen countless battles, and has learnt many ways to savagely hunt down the foes he faces.*

Add 1 to the number of command points you start the battle with.

Bellowing Carnosaur: *Even the most dauntless enemies turn tail and flee in the presence of Ku-Quar's monstrous mount.*

Add 1 to the dice roll when using Ku-Quar's Bloodroar ability.

WARSCROLL BATTALION
DRACOTHION'S TAIL

Whipping across the heavens, the tail of the great star drake Dracothion is said to mirror the mood of Azyr itself. Within the stars of this vast constellation dwell the armies of the Scar-Veteran Quar-Toc, known as the Fury of Azyr. They appear at the call of the Slann Starmaster Kuoteq, riding and flying forth from the stars and into the Mortal Realms. As befits the constellation from which they come, the seraphon of Dracothion's Tail are quick and unpredictable upon the battlefield, and their ranks are filled with Saurus Knights, Ripperdactyls and Terradon Riders.

ORGANISATION

A Dracothion's Tail battalion consists of the following:

- 1 Slann Starmaster (Kuoteq)

- 1 Firelance Starhost battalion

A Dracothion's Tail battalion may also contain:

- 0-4 warscroll battalions chosen in any combination from the following list:

  - Sunclaw Starhost

  - Firelance Starhost

  - Eternal Starhost

  - Shadowstrike Starhost

- Any number of additional **SERAPHON** units

If a Dracothion's Tail battalion contains the maximum number of battalions, it gains the Strategic Mastery ability from the Starbeast Constellation warscroll battalion in *Battletome: Seraphon*.

ABILITIES

Appear at Kuoteq's Command: *At the will of their Starmaster, the reptilian throngs of Dracothion's Tail appear on the battlefield, emerging from beams of starlight to savage their foes.*

Instead of setting up a unit from this battalion on the battlefield, you can place it to one side and say that it is set up waiting to appear at Kuoteq's command as a reserve unit. You can set up one reserve unit waiting to appear at Kuoteq's command for each unit from the same battalion you set up on the battlefield.

In your hero phase, you can set up one or more of the reserve units waiting to appear at Kuoteq's command on the battlefield more than 9" from any enemy units and wholly within 18" of Kuoteq. However, each reserve unit set up in the same turn must be a different unit chosen from a different warscroll – Kuoteq cannot command the same unit to appear more than once in the same turn. Reserve units that are set up on the battlefield for the first time cannot move in the following movement phase. Any reserve units waiting to appear at Kuoteq's command which are not set up on the battlefield before the start of the fourth battle round are slain.

ALLEGIANCE ABILITIES
WANDERERS

This section describes the allegiance abilities available to a Wanderers army, including battle traits for the army, command traits for its general and the artefacts of power available to its heroes.

BATTLE TRAITS

Defiant Hunters: *Wanderers are undaunted by the savagery of the realms and will let no misfortune deter them from their path.*

You can re-roll battleshock tests for friendly **WANDERERS** units.

Realm Wanderers: *These aelves, as their name implies, have travelled the realms for generations and know many hidden paths.*

At the start of your movement phase, one friendly **WANDERERS** unit wholly within 6" of the edge of the battlefield can leave to travel along a hidden pathway instead of making a move. If they do so, remove the unit from the battlefield. Then set the unit up, anywhere wholly within 6" of the edge of the battlefield by which it left, and more than 9" from any enemy models. This counts as that unit's move for that movement phase.

Melt Away: *Wanderers are impossibly difficult to lock in combat, melting away to strike from afar with their missile weapons.*

Friendly **WANDERERS** units can retreat and shoot in the same turn.

COMMAND TRAITS

D6   Command Trait

1   **Stalker of the Hidden Paths:** *This general knows well the geomantic lines that connect the battlefields of the Mortal Realms.*

If a friendly **WANDERER** unit wholly within 12" of this general leaves the battlefield using the Realm Wanderers battle trait, it can return wholly within 6" of any edge of the battlefield, not just the one it left by, and more than 9" from any enemy models. This counts as that unit's move for that movement phase.

2   **Myst Walker:** *Eldritch fog enshrouds this aelf, hiding them from the prying eyes and vicious blades of the enemy.*

Enemy units can only attack this general if it is the closest enemy model when the attack is made.

3   **Masterful Hunter:** *Volleys loosed by this aelf fly unerringly towards their targets, striking where there are gaps in armour and piercing vital organs.*

Add 1 to hit rolls for attacks made with this general's missile weapons. If this general does not have a missile weapon, they receive a Hunting Hawk instead, and can use Hunting Hawk's Beak missile weapon from the Nomad Prince warscroll.

4   **Eagle-eyed:** *No matter how far their quarry runs, this general is able to track them and strike them down.*

Add 10" to the Range characteristic of missile weapons used by this general. If this general does not have a missile weapon, they receive a Hunting Hawk instead, and can use Hunting Hawk's Beak missile weapon from the Nomad Prince warscroll.

5   **Lord of Blades:** *At close-quarters, this noble aelf is a paragon of battle, sweeping deftly past their foes defences to deliver the killing blow.*

You can re-roll hit rolls of 1 for this general's melee weapons.

6   **Singer of Spells:** *When this general speaks they form beauteous harmonies, their musical words mixing with the winds of magic.*

Add 1 to this general's casting and unbinding rolls if they are a **WIZARD**. If they are not a **WIZARD**, they gain the **WIZARD** keyword, and can attempt to unbind one spell in each enemy hero phase (but note that they cannot attempt to cast any spells).

ARTEFACTS OF POWER

D6	Artefact

1   **Falcon of Holthaven:** *This territorial raptor guarded the tomb of its first master for centuries, and to this day it harries those who would despoil its domain.*

Roll a dice each time an enemy unit ends a normal move within 12" of the bearer. On a 4+ that unit suffers 1 mortal wound.

2   **Starcaster Longbow:** *In place of a bowstring, a ley line runs between the limbs of this bow, and when plucked it looses solid shards of Sigendil's light.*

In your shooting phase, you can pick an enemy unit within 20" of the bearer and roll a dice. On a 2-5 that unit suffers 1 mortal wound; on a 6+ that unit suffers D3 mortal wounds.

3   **Splinterbirch Blade:** *When struck against armour, this blade of still-living wood shatters into thousands of needle-sharp shards only to re-grow itself instantly.*

Pick one of the bearer's melee weapons. Improve the Rend characteristic of that weapon by 1.

4   **Wending Wand:** *Used by the Wanderers as a dowsing rod, the leaves on this supple branch twitch in the winds that course along ley lines.*

Once per battle, a unit returning to the battlefield after using the Realm Wanderers battle trait can be set up wholly within 18" of the bearer, wholly within 6" of any edge of the battlefield, not just the one it left by, and more than 9" from any enemy models. This counts as that unit's move for that movement phase.

5   **Viridescent Shawl:** *Depending on the mood of its wearer, this cloak can exude the lushness of an emerald glade or the choking dark of a briar thicket.*

Add 1 to casting rolls for friendly **WANDERER WIZARDS** within 9" of the bearer. In addition, subtract 1 from hit rolls for missile weapons that target the bearer.

6   **Forget-me-knot:** *When bound by this chain of delicate florets, the unsuspecting victim sees themselves not on the battlefield, but in an endless confluence of ethereal paths.*

Once per battle, at the start of the combat phase, pick an enemy **HERO** within 3" of the bearer. That **HERO** cannot fight or use abilities in that combat phase.

ALLEGIANCE ABILITIES
BRAYHERD

This section describes the allegiance abilities available to a Brayherd army, including battle traits for the army, command traits for its general and the artefacts of power available to its heroes.

BATTLE TRAITS

Ambush: *Endowed with the cunning of the hunting pack, Beastmen are adept at encircling the enemy and attacking from an unexpected direction.*

Instead of setting up a **BRAYHERD** unit on the battlefield, you can set it up hiding in ambush. At the end of your first movement phase you must set up all ambushing units, wholly within 6" of the edge of the battlefield, and more than 9" from any enemy models.

Herdstones: *Herdstones are sacred to the Brayherds, and all manner of offerings are left there to appease the gods, from weapons, armour and the banners of vanquished foes, to the corpses of mutilated enemies.*

After set-up is complete, but before the battle begins, you can set up a herdstone wholly within your territory. Use a suitable terrain feature up to 4" across to represent the herdstone. It must be set up on an area of open ground more than 1" from any models, terrain features or objectives.

Friendly **BRAYHERD** units treat a herdstone as having the Damned, Arcane and Inspiring scenery rules; enemy units treat a herdstone as having the Deadly scenery rule instead.

COMMAND TRAITS

D6	Command Trait

1 Unreasoning and Deadly: *This general craves nothing save the carnage of battle and the butchery of its enemies.*

Re-roll wound rolls of 1 for this general.

2 Crown of Horns: *This beastman gouges and gores its foes with the gnarled antlers that sprout from its skull.*

When this general is picked to fight in the combat phase, pick an enemy unit within 1" of them and roll a dice. On a 5 that unit suffers 1 mortal wound; on a 6+ that unit suffers D3 mortal wounds.

3 Malevolent Despoiler: *To this spiteful creature, the lush forests and robust buildings of the Mortal Realms exist only to be torn down.*

Do not add 1 to the save roll of enemy units that are in cover while they are within 12" of this general.

4 Massive Beastlord: *This beastman towers above others of its kin, and will fight on through even the most grievous wounds.*

Add 1 to this general's Wounds characteristic.

5 Scion of the Dark Gods: *Blessed with the favour of the Ruinous Powers, this general unleashes fell energies upon the Mortal Realms.*

If this general is a **WIZARD**, add 1 to their casting rolls in the hero phase. If they are not a **WIZARD**, they gain the **WIZARD** keyword, and can attempt to cast Arcane Bolt or Mystic Shield in their hero phase (but cannot attempt to cast any other spell or unbind spells in the enemy hero phase).

6 Bestial Cunning: *Guided by predatory instincts, this general moves its herds to surround and outflank the armies of the enemy.*

Up to half of the units that are set up hiding in Ambush (see battle traits), rounding fractions up, can arrive in your second movement phase.

ARTEFACTS OF POWER

D6   Artefact

1   Ramhorn Helm: *The curving horns on this headdress spiral around the wearer's own, allowing them to deliver a devastating headbutt to any enemy that lowers its guard.*

After the bearer completes a charge move, pick an enemy unit within 1" of them. That unit suffers D3 mortal wounds.

2   Brayblast Trumpet: *Carved from Shaggoth bone, this horn sends its thunderous blasts across the Mortal Realms, drawing towards it the most savage children of the Chaos Gods.*

Add 1 to hit rolls for friendly **BRAYHERD** units wholly within 18" of the bearer if those units used the Ambush battle trait to set up on the battlefield in that turn.

3   Herdstone Axe: *The jagged blade of this stone axe is said to have been sheared from the largest herdstone in the Mortal Realms, and it glows with the sickly light of Chaos magic.*

Pick one of the bearer's melee weapons. Add 1 to that weapon's Damage characteristic.

4   Bleating Gnarlstaff: *Infused with the warping taint of Chaos, the bestial shrieks of this twisted branch cause stones and plants to awaken with animal fury.*

Roll a dice if the bearer is within 1" of a terrain feature at the end of your movement phase. On a 3+ each enemy unit within 1" of that terrain feature suffers 1 mortal wound.

5   The Festerpelt: *Matted and maggot-riddled, this pulsating fur binds to the hide of only the most vile gore-kin and re-knits their wounds with mouldering sinews.*

At the start your hero phase, heal 1 wound that has been allocated to the bearer.

6   Rune of the Insatiable Beast: *Marked from birth with this crescent-shaped deformity, this creature is consumed with an unquenchable hunger for the clangour of battle.*

Add 2 to charge rolls for the bearer. In addition, you can re-roll hit rolls of 1 for the bearer.

ALLEGIANCE ABILITIES
SLAANESH

This section describes the allegiance abilities available to a Slaanesh army, including battle traits for the army, command traits for its general and the artefacts of power available to its heroes.

BATTLE TRAITS

The Hosts: *The disappearance of Slaanesh has divided his followers into several factions, each with their own goals and methods of fighting.*

After set-up is complete, but before the battle begins, choose one of the following hosts for the army to belong to. The rules for that host apply to all friendly **SLAANESH** units for the duration of the battle.

Pretenders: The general of a Pretenders host has two different command traits rather than only one. If you randomly generate the traits, roll again if the second result is the same as the first. In addition, you can re-roll hit rolls of 1 for melee and missile weapons used by friendly Pretenders units that have ten or more models when they are selected to shoot or fight.

Seekers: Add 1" to the Move characteristic and charge moves of all models in a Seekers host. Add 2" instead if the model's original Move characteristic is 10" or more. In addition, units in the host that are within 12" of the enemy in the charge phase must attempt to charge if able to do so, and the first model from the unit that is moved must finish the charge move within ½" of an enemy model if its charge move is high enough for it to do so.

Invaders: An Invaders host can have up to three generals rather than only one. Only one of the generals (your choice) can have a command trait, but all three are considered to be a general when you use a command ability. However, the generals cannot use a command trait or be chosen as the model from which a command ability is measured while they are within 12" of any of the other generals – they are too busy hurling insults at their rival.

Feed on Depravity: *Through the indulgence of forbidden violence and excess, the walls of reality can be weakened and made thin enough to draw forth Slaaneshi daemons from the Realm of Chaos.*

You can summon units of **SLAANESH DAEMONS** to the battlefield if you collect enough Depravity Points. Each time a friendly **SLAANESH HERO** inflicts a wound on an enemy model but that model is not slain by that wound you receive 1 Depravity Point. In addition, every time a wound is inflicted on a friendly **SLAANESH HERO** but that model is not slain by that wound you receive 1 Depravity Point.

For example, in the combat phase a Keeper of Secrets inflicts 10 damage upon a unit of 5 Stormcast Liberators. As the Liberators each have a Wounds characteristic of 2, the first wound allocated to each Liberator in turn generates a Depravity Point. The second wound allocated to each Liberator in turn does not generate a Depravity Point as the model is slain, so the Slaanesh player generates 5 Depravity Points in total.

If you have 6 or more Depravity Points at the end of your movement phase, you can summon one or more units from the list on the right onto the battlefield, and add them to your army. Each unit you summon costs a number of Depravity Points, as shown on the list, and you can only summon a unit if you have enough Depravity Points to pay its cost.

Summoned units must be set up wholly within 12" of a friendly **SLAANESH HERO** and more than 9" from any enemy units. Subtract the cost of the summoned unit from the number of Depravity Points you have immediately after it has been set up.

DAEMONS OF SLAANESH UNIT	COST
1 Keeper of Secrets	24
3 Seeker Chariots of Slaanesh	24
20 Daemonettes	18
1 Herald of Slaanesh on Exalted Seeker Chariot	18
10 Daemonettes of Slaanesh	12
1 Exalted Seeker Chariot of Slaanesh	12
3 Fiends of Slaanesh	12
1 Hellflayer of Slaanesh	12
1 Herald of Slaanesh on Seeker Chariot	12
1 Seeker Chariot of Slaanesh	12
5 Seekers of Slaanesh	12
5 Daemonettes of Slaanesh	6
1 Herald of Slaanesh	6

COMMAND TRAITS

D6   **Command Trait**

1   **Lord of Excess:** *The servants of Slaanesh are enthralled by this warlord's flamboyant kills.*

At the start of the battleshock phase, add the number of models slain by attacks made by this general during this turn to the Bravery characteristic of friendly **SLAANESH** units that are wholly within 12" of this general. The bonus lasts until the end of that battleshock phase.

2   **Devotee of Torment:** *This general is ever eager to inflict more pain on their enemies.*

This general can pile in 6" instead of 3". In addition, this general can be picked to fight in the combat phase if they are within 6" of an enemy unit, rather than only 3".

3   **Invigorated by Pain:** *The sadism of this general knows no bounds, and with every cruel wound they inflict upon their foes they are reinvigorated.*

Roll a dice each time this general inflicts a wound on an enemy unit. On a 6+, heal 1 wound that has been allocated to this general.

4   **Supremely Vain:** *This egomaniacal tyrant craves admiration, and is quick to showcase their depraved talents when an audience of their followers is present.*

Add 1 to hit rolls, casting rolls and unbinding rolls for this general if there are 10 or more friendly **SLAANESH** models within 6" of this general when the roll is made.

5   **Allure of Slaanesh:** *The perverse beauty with which this general is possessed deadens the senses of all who approach them.*

Subtract 1 from hit rolls for attacks made by melee weapons that target this general.

6   **Cruel and Sadistic:** *The horrendous manner in which this servant of Slaanesh goes about their slaughter sends waves of fear through even the most dauntless opponents.*

Enemy units must add 2 to their battleshock rolls for each model slain by attacks made by this general with a melee weapon, instead of only 1.

ARTEFACTS OF POWER

D6	Artefact

1 Lash of Despair: *The cords of this whip are spun soul-stuff, and when the lash cracks the soul-streamers splay outward, striking wildly at all nearby.*

At the start of your shooting phase, roll a dice for each enemy unit within 6" of the bearer. On a 4+ that unit suffers 1 mortal wound.

2 Breathtaker: *Laced with ornate filigrees and capable of moving with unnatural grace, this blade captivates those it strikes and saps their will to retaliate.*

At the start of the combat phase, pick an enemy unit within 3" of the bearer and roll a dice. On a 3+ that unit cannot be picked to fight until all other eligible enemy units have fought.

3 Mask of Spiteful Beauty: *This mask fills the souls of those who behold it with disgust at their own grotesque appearance.*

At the start of your hero phase, pick an enemy unit within 6" of the bearer. Subtract 2 from that unit's Bravery characteristic until your next hero phase.

4 Enrapturing Circlet: *The variegated tendrils exuded by this daemonic band form inescapable coils around the hardened souls of warriors.*

At the start of your hero phase, enemy units within 3" of the bearer suffer 1 mortal wound. In addition, enemy units within 3" of the bearer at the start of your opponent's movement phase cannot retreat that phase.

5 Icon of Infinite Excess: *Slaanesh's most opulent standard drives both the followers and enemies of the Dark Prince into orgiastic fits of violence.*

Once per battle, at the start of the combat phase, the bearer can use this artefact. If they do so, until the end of that combat phase, add 1 to hit rolls for models that were within 8" of the bearer at the start of that combat phase.

6 Fallacious Gift: *To the beholder, this cursed frippery appears to be a sacred weapon that must be acquired, not the creation of a cruel god that it truly is.*

After set-up is complete, but before the battle begins, pick one enemy **Hero**, and then pick one of their weapons. At the end of each battle round in which they attacked with that weapon, that **Hero** suffers 1 mortal wound.

ALLEGIANCE ABILITIES
SLAVES TO DARKNESS

This section describes the allegiance abilities available to a Slaves to Darkness army, including battle traits for the army, command traits for its general and the artefacts of power available to its heroes.

BATTLE TRAITS

Aura of Chaos Power: *The Champions of the Chaos Gods can grant some of the power they receive to their followers.*

Khorne: You can re-roll hit rolls of 1 for attacks with melee weapons used by friendly **KHORNE SLAVE TO DARKNESS** units while they are wholly within 8" of a friendly **KHORNE SLAVES TO DARKNESS HERO**.

Slaanesh: You can re-roll run and charge rolls for friendly **SLAANESH SLAVE TO DARKNESS** units that are wholly within 6" of a friendly **SLAANESH SLAVES TO DARKNESS HERO** when the roll is made.

Nurgle: You can re-roll wound rolls of 1 for attacks made by friendly **NURGLE SLAVE TO DARKNESS** units while they are wholly within 7" of a friendly **NURGLE SLAVES TO DARKNESS HERO**.

Tzeentch: You can re-roll save rolls of 1 for friendly **TZEENTCH SLAVE TO DARKNESS** units while they are wholly within 9" of a friendly **TZEENTCH SLAVES TO DARKNESS HERO**.

No Mark: Add 1 to the Bravery characteristic of friendly **SLAVE TO DARKNESS** units that do not have a **KHORNE, NURGLE, SLAANESH** or **TZEENTCH** keyword while they are wholly within 12" of a friendly **SLAVES TO DARKNESS HERO** that does not have a **KHORNE, NURGLE, SLAANESH** or **TZEENTCH** keyword.

Eye of the Gods: *The Ruinous Powers grant their champions gifts that make the faithful mighty indeed.*

If a friendly **SLAVES TO DARKNESS HERO** (excluding a **DAEMON PRINCE**) makes an attack with a melee weapon that slays one or more enemy **HEROES** or **MONSTERS**, make a roll on the Eye of the Gods table (below) after your hero's attacks have been completed.

If your hero receives a reward that it already has, roll a dice. On a 1-3 your hero receives the 'Spawndom' reward instead, and on a 4-6 they receive the 'Dark Apotheosis' reward instead.

EYE OF THE GODS

2D6	Reward
2	**Spawndom:** You can add a **CHAOS SPAWN** to your army. If you do so, set up a **CHAOS SPAWN** model within 1" of this **HERO**, and then remove this **HERO**. The **CHAOS SPAWN** cannot fight in the phase in which it is set up. If you do not add a **CHAOS SPAWN** to your army, this **HERO** suffers D3 mortal wounds instead.
3-4	**Unholy Resilience:** Add 1 to this **HERO**'s Wounds characteristic for the rest of the battle.
5	**Iron Skin:** Add 1 to save rolls for this **HERO** for the rest of the battle.
6-8	**The Eye Opens:** You can re-roll the next failed hit, wound or save roll for this **HERO**.
9	**Murderous Mutation:** Add 1 to hit rolls for this **HERO** for the rest of the battle.
10-11	**Slaughterer's Strength:** Add 1 to wound rolls for this **HERO** for the rest of the battle.
12	**Dark Apotheosis:** You can add a **DAEMON PRINCE** to your army. If you do, set up a **DAEMON PRINCE** model within 1" of this **HERO**, and then remove this **HERO**. The **DAEMON PRINCE** cannot attack in the phase in which it is set up. If you do not add a **DAEMON PRINCE** to your army, heal D3 wounds allocated to this **HERO** instead.

COMMAND TRAITS

D6	Command Trait

1 **Eternal Vendetta:** *Burning in the chest of this general is an undying hatred for the followers of Sigmar's Pantheon.*

You can re-roll failed wound rolls for this general's melee weapons if the target has the **ORDER** keyword.

2 **Flames of Spite:** *Chaotic fire clings to the form of this warlord, leaping out to immolate those who have earned their ire.*

If the wound roll for an attack made by this general is 6+, the target suffers 1 mortal wound in addition to any other damage the attack inflicts.

3 **Master of Deception:** *This dishonourable champion sees into the minds of their enemies, and uses guile and trickery to wrong-foot them.*

Subtract 1 from hit rolls for attacks made with melee weapons that target this general.

4 **Hatred Incarnate:** *This general is imbued with an unnatural loathing that manifests as a crackling corona of Chaos energy.*

You can re-roll wound rolls of 1 for attacks made by this general.

5 **Lord of Terror:** *Where this champion walks, the inhuman howls of daemonic entities follow them, striking horror into the hearts of all in their path.*

Subtract 1 from the Bravery characteristic of enemy units while they are within 6" of this general.

6 **Exalted Champion:** *This warlord is a paragon amongst the mortal servants of the Chaos Gods, and a living idol to those who follow them.*

Add 1 to the Bravery characteristic of friendly **SLAVES TO DARKNESS** units while they are wholly within 12" of this general.

ARTEFACTS OF POWER

D6	Artefact

1 **Hellfire Sword:** *This blade was made from a single, searing flame that was hammered into material form and quenched in the blood of a fire-djinn.*

Once per battle, in your shooting phase, pick an enemy unit within 8" of the bearer. That unit suffers D3 mortal wounds.

2 **Idolatrous Plackart:** *The profane inscriptions and grim fetishes adorning this breastplate project an unholy aura to provide the most devout Chaos worshippers with daemonic resilience.*

Roll a dice each time a mortal wound is allocated to the bearer. On a 5+ the mortal wound is negated.

3 **Helm of the Oppressor:** *The blackened bone plates of this helmet induce a soul-piercing dread in the Chaos champion's enemies.*

Subtract 2 from the Bravery characteristic of enemy units while they are within 6" of the bearer.

4 **Banner of the Demagogue:** *Those who flock to this banner are enraptured by the hypnotic words of the one who waves it, believing false promises that they too will have lasting glory.*

Add 2 to the Bravery characteristic of friendly **SLAVES TO DARKNESS** units while they are wholly within 12" of the bearer.

5 **Mark of the All-favoured:** *The blessings of all four ruinous powers hang equally thick around this unholy mutation.*

The bearer has the **KHORNE**, **NURGLE**, **SLAANESH** and **TZEENTCH** keywords.

6 **Desecrator Gauntlets:** *The coruscant energies that crackle around these paired iron gloves corrupts and destroys that which is sacred or imbued with magic.*

Subtract 2 from the casting rolls of enemy **WIZARDS** while they are within 3" of the bearer. In addition, add 1 to wound rolls for attacks made by the bearer if the target is a **WIZARD** or **PRIEST**.

ALLEGIANCE ABILITIES
SKAVEN PESTILENS

This section describes the allegiance abilities available to a Skaven Pestilens army, including battle traits for the army, command traits for its general and the artefacts of power available to its heroes.

BATTLE TRAITS

Strength in Numbers: *Skaven are not brave by nature, but do take courage from being in large packs.*

When a **SKAVEN PESTILENS** unit takes a battleshock test, add 2 instead of 1 to its Bravery characteristic for every 10 models in the unit.

Echoes of the Great Plagues: *Sometimes the prayers of Pestilens priests cause the effects of one of the Great Plagues to temporarily manifest upon the battlefield.*

When a **PESTILENS PRIEST** successfully prays, and the dice roll for the prayer was a 6 before any modifiers were applied, you can pick one of the following Great Plagues to manifest as well as using one of the prayers on the **PRIEST'S** warscroll. Each Great Plague can manifest once per battle, and no more than one can manifest per turn.

Redmaw Plague: The nearest enemy **HERO** within 13" of the **PRIEST** is infected with the Redmaw Plague. If that **HERO** is within 3" of models from its own army at the start of any combat phase, and not within 3" of any models from your army, then it will attack its friends – treat that **HERO** as a model from your army for the rest of that combat phase.

The Neverplague: Add 1 to prayer rolls for friendly **PESTILENS PRIESTS** for the rest of the battle.

Bubonic Blightplague: The nearest enemy unit within 13" of the **PRIEST** is infected with the Bubonic Blightplague. That unit suffers D6 mortal wounds. If the unit is destroyed when these wounds are allocated, pick another enemy unit within 6" of the last model to be removed from the infected unit. The new unit suffers D3 mortal wounds. If the second unit is also destroyed,

then the Blightplague inflicts D3 mortal wounds on another enemy unit, and so on until a unit is not destroyed by the disease, or there are no other units within range when a unit is destroyed.

Undulant Scourge: The nearest enemy model within 13" of the **PRIEST** is infected by the Undulant Scourge. The infected model's unit suffers 1 mortal wound, plus 1 extra mortal wound for each other model from the unit that is within 3" of the infected model.

Crimsonweal Curse: The nearest enemy unit within 13" of the **PRIEST** is infected by the Crimsonweal Curse. The infected unit suffers 1 mortal wound. In addition, the infected unit, and each enemy unit within 1" of the infected unit, suffers 1 mortal wound in each of your future hero phases.

COMMAND TRAITS

D6	Command Trait
1	**Malevolent:** *Spite and hatred drive this warlord to ever fouler acts of violence.* You can re-roll wound rolls of 1 for attacks made by this general.
2	**Diseased:** *Those who draw too close to this plague-infested rat are consumed by infection.* Roll a dice if this general is within 3" of any enemy units at the start of your hero phase. On a 5+ inflict D3 mortal wounds on one enemy unit that is within 3" of this general.
3	**Master of Rot and Ruin:** *This general's presence heralds the coming of the Great Plagues.* If this general is a **PRIEST**, you can re-roll the dice when they pray. If they are not a **PRIEST**, they gain the **PRIEST** keyword and can use the Pestilent Prayers ability from the Plague Priest warscroll.
4	**Fanatical Leader:** *This general falls upon their enemies in a thrashing, frothing frenzy.* Add 1 to the Attacks characteristic of this general's melee weapons.
5	**Verminous Valour:** *This foetid rat inspires many martyrs amongst their followers.* Each time you allocate a wound or mortal wound to this general, you can roll a dice. On a 4+ the wound is negated but you must inflict 1 mortal wound on a friendly **PESTILENS** unit within 3" of this general instead.
6	**Architect of Death:** *A rain of projectile putrescence precedes this general's advance.* You can re-roll wound rolls of 1 for attacks made with missile weapons by friendly **PESTILENS** units while they are wholly within 12" of this general.

ARTEFACTS OF POWER

D6   Artefact

1   The Fumigatous: *When a name is spoken while this ornate censor is being swung, the cloud of pungent toxins coalesces and seeks out the one who possesses that name.*

At the start of each combat phase, pick an enemy unit within 6" of the bearer. On a 3+ that unit suffers 1 mortal wound.

2   Brooding Blade: *Those wounded by this filth-encrusted dagger become host to dozens of plague-bearing rats, who burrow outward through their victim's flesh before spreading disease to those nearby.*

Pick one of the bearer's melee weapons. At the end of the combat phase, roll a dice for each unit that suffered any wounds inflicted by that weapon. On a 6+ that unit also suffers D3 mortal wounds.

3   Bilious Bell: *Each peal of this bell sends waves of crippling nausea through those in earshot. As the chiming grows louder, the afflicted start vomiting great spouts of curdled ichor.*

In your hero phase, roll a dice for each enemy unit within 12" of the bearer. On a roll of 4+ subtract 1 from the Bravery characteristic of that unit until your next hero phase.

4   Blistrevous, the Living Cyst: *This sentient pustule migrates from host to host, whispering its mad ravings to drive its bearer into a fevered frenzy.*

You can re-roll hit rolls of 1 for attacks made by the bearer, and add 2" to the bearer's Move characteristic. Starting from the second battle round, at the start of your hero phase, if there are any friendly PESTILENS HEROES within 12" of the bearer, you must transfer this artefact to one of them.

5   Liber Bubonicus: *This foul book is inscribed with the secrets of every pestilence in the Mortal Realms.*

The bearer can use the Pestilent Prayers ability from the Plague Priest warscroll. If the bearer is a PLAGUE PRIEST, then it can use the Pestilent Prayers ability twice in your hero phase.

6   Vexler's Shroud: *Laced with delicate shards of warpstone, this cowl casts an impenetrable shadow over its wearer, and all who look upon it are consumed by the plague of darkness.*

Subtract 1 from hit rolls for attacks made with missile weapons that target the bearer.

ALLEGIANCE ABILITIES
SKAVEN SKRYRE

This section describes the allegiance abilities available to a Skaven Skryre army, including battle traits for the army, command traits for its general and the artefacts of power available to its heroes.

BATTLE TRAITS

Strength in Numbers: *Skaven are not brave by nature, but do take courage from being in large packs.*

When a **SKAVEN SKRYRE** unit takes a battleshock test, add 2 instead of 1 to its Bravery characteristic for every 10 models in the unit.

Warpstone Sparks: *These pieces of refined warpstone are used to aid spellcasting and improve the potency of skaven weapons. The use of warpstone sparks is dangerous, but the quick road to power is an irresistible lure for any skaven.*

At the start of the battle, before either army is set up, roll a D3 and add 3 to the roll. The result is the number of warpstone sparks that you can use during the battle. Keep track of these with small counters.

Each time you use a warpstone spark, discard one of your warpstone spark counters. Each warpstone spark can be used once per battle and you cannot use more than one warpstone spark in the same phase.

Roll a dice after using a warpstone spark and resolving the spell or attack it was used to affect. On a 1 the unit that cast the spell or made the attack suffers D3 mortal wounds.

Each warpstone spark can be used to do one of the following:

- Re-roll a casting roll or unbinding roll for a friendly **SKRYRE WIZARD**.

- Re-roll a failed hit or wound roll for an attack made by a friendly **SKRYRE HERO**.

- Add 1 to the Damage characteristic of a weapon used by a friendly **SKRYRE** model that has made a successful attack.

You must decide if you want to re-roll a roll immediately after making it.

COMMAND TRAITS

D6	Command Trait
1	**Malevolent:** *Spite and hatred drive this warlord to ever fouler acts of violence.* You can re-roll wound rolls of 1 for attacks made by this general.
2	**Cunning Creature:** *This skaven has not lived as long as it has due to honour or valour, but instead due to its masterful skills of self-preservation.* When this general fights, instead of piling in and attacking, they can withdraw instead. Move this general up to 8", so that they end the move more than 3" away from any enemy models.
3	**Deranged Inventor:** *The fell contraptions created by this general are beyond compare in terms of lethality and derangement.* You can re-roll failed hit rolls for attacks made by friendly **SKRYRE WAR MACHINES** while they are within 6" of this general.
4	**Masterful Scavenger:** *This avaricious rat has amassed a great horde of warpstone which they use to terrifying effect on their enemies.* This general's army starts the battle with D3 extra warpstone sparks (see battle traits).
5	**Verminous Valour:** *This insidious rat inspires many martyrs amongst their followers.* Each time you allocate a wound or mortal wound to this general, you can roll a dice. On a 4+ the wound is negated but you must inflict 1 mortal wound on a friendly **SKRYRE** unit within 3" of this general instead.
6	**Overseer of Destruction:** *Gouts of flame and clouds of poisoned gas are the signatures of this keen general.* You can re-roll hit rolls of 1 for attacks made by friendly **SKRYRE WEAPON TEAMS** while they are wholly within 12" of this general.

ARTEFACTS OF POWER

D6   Artefact

1   Assassins-bane Rig: *Hidden inside the latches and cogwork buckles of this body harness are dozens of switchblades and serrated warpshards to cut down would-be killers.*

At the end of the combat phase, roll a dice for each enemy unit within 3" of the bearer that made any attacks on the bearer. On a 3+ that unit suffers 1 mortal wound.

2   Esoteric Warp Resonator: *As each of the thirteen dials are rotated, the stored warpstone energy inside this sealed orb causes it to quiver and glow.*

You can use one warpstone spark each turn for the bearer without having to discard any warpstone spark counters.

3   Skryre's-breath Bellows: *Fitted with warpstone-powered turbines, these bellows blow plumes of poisoned wind across friend and foe alike.*

At the start of your hero phase, roll a dice for each unit within 3" of the bearer (excluding the bearer). On a 5+ that unit suffers D3 mortal wounds.

4   Vial of the Fulminator: *The highly combustible oil within this vial is the perfect fuel for explosively accelerating Skryre war machines across the battlefield.*

At the start of your movement phase, pick a friendly **SKRYRE WAR MACHINE** unit within 3" of the bearer. You can double that unit's Move characteristic until the end of the phase. However, if you do, that unit suffers 1 mortal wound at the end of that phase.

5   Vigordust Injector: *The shards of pulverised toxins administered by this syringe cause injected skaven to froth at the mouth as they enter a violent and extremely painful frenzy before dying.*

In your hero phase, pick a friendly **SKRYRE** unit wholly within 12" of the bearer. Add 1 to charge rolls and hit rolls for that unit until your next hero phase. However, at the start of your next hero phase that unit suffers D3 mortal wounds.

6   Brass Orb: *A fist-sized metal orb made of interlinking cogs, the Brass Orb is a dangerous device capable of opening a sucking crack in the plane of reality.*

Once per battle, at the start of your hero phase, roll a dice. On a 6+ the closest enemy model within 6" of the bearer is slain.

ALLEGIANCE ABILITIES
FLESH-EATER COURTS

This section describes the allegiance abilities available to a Flesh-eater Courts army, including battle traits for the army, command traits for its general and the artefacts of power available to its heroes.

BATTLE TRAITS

Deathless Courtiers: *The demented followers of a Flesh-eater king consider themselves beyond the reach of death when they linger in his shadow, their sundered flesh re-knitting in an instant.*

Each time you allocate a wound or mortal wound to a friendly **Flesh-eater Courts** unit while they are wholly within 12" of your general or a friendly **Flesh-eater Courts Hero**, roll a dice. On a 6+ the wound is negated.

Feeding Frenzy: *The followers of the Ghoul-kings hunger for flesh, and consuming it can drive them into a gore-fuelled frenzy.*

In the combat phase, after a friendly **Flesh-eater Courts** unit has made all of its attacks, roll a dice if the attacks made by that unit resulted in any enemy units being destroyed. On a 6+ that **Flesh-eater Courts** unit can fight for a second time. The result of this fight will not allow the unit to fight again, even if it results in another enemy unit being destroyed.

Courts of Delusion: *The warriors that make up a Flesh-eater Court believe themselves noble soldiers serving a glorious king.*

After set-up is complete, but before the battle begins, choose or roll for a delusion from the table below. The rules for that grudge apply to all friendly **Flesh-eater Courts** units for the duration of the battle.

D6	Delusion
1	**Crusading Army:** You can re-roll run or charge rolls for friendly **Flesh-eater Courts** units.
2	**The Royal Hunt:** You can re-roll hit and wound rolls of 1 for friendly **Flesh-eater Courts** units if the target is a **Monster**.
3	**The Feast Day:** You can re-roll dice rolls of 1 when rolling to see if a friendly **Flesh-eater Courts** unit becomes subject to a feeding frenzy (see above).
4	**A Matter of Honour:** You can re-roll hit rolls of 1 for friendly **Flesh-eater Courts** units if the target is a **Hero**. If the target is the enemy army's general, you can re-roll wound rolls of 1 as well.
5	**The Grand Tournament:** You can re-roll hit rolls of 1 for friendly **Flesh-eater Courts Heroes** other than your general.
6	**Defenders of the Realm:** You can re-roll save rolls of 1 for friendly **Flesh-eater Courts** units while they are wholly within your territory.

COMMAND TRAITS

D6	Command Trait

1   **Bringer of Death:** *This general sees every enemy as a wretch that must be put out of its misery.*

You can re-roll wound rolls of 1 for attacks made by this general.

2   **Frenzied Flesh-eater:** *The taste of warm blood spurs this ghoulish creature into a frenzy.*

You can re-roll failed hit rolls for attacks made by this general while they are subject to a feeding frenzy (see battle traits).

3   **Majestic Horror:** *The champion's grim regality draws countless cannibalistic warriors to his banner.*

If this general is chosen as the model that uses a command ability that summons **FLESH-EATER COURTS** models to the battlefield, they can use it twice in succession without a command point having to be spent the second time. If they do not have such a command ability, they can use the Summon Men-at-arms ability from the Abhorrant Ghoul King warscroll.

4   **Savage Beyond Reason:** *In his deluded state, this general no longer remembers what sleight to his honour drove him to such rage.*

Add 1 to the dice roll to see if this general becomes subject to a feeding frenzy (see battle traits).

5   **Dark Wizardry:** *An aura of necromantic energy hangs thick around this creature.*

If this general is a **WIZARD**, add 1 to casting and unbinding rolls for them. If this general is not a **WIZARD**, they gain the **WIZARD** keyword and can cast and unbind spells in the same manner as an **ABHORRANT GHOUL KING** from the Abhorrant Ghoul King warscroll.

6   **Completely Delusional:** *The followers of this general see all that is in his mind's eye.*

Once per battle, if this general has not been slain, you can you can pick a new delusion in your hero phase to replace the original delusion you chose for your army (see battle traits).

ARTEFACTS OF POWER

D6	Artefact

1   **The Flayed Pennant:** *The wind carries the waft of fresh blood from this dripping flag, sending the denizens of the Flesh-eater Courts into a frenzy.*

Once per battle, at the start of your charge phase, the bearer can use this artefact. If they do so, friendly **FLESH-EATER COURTS** units wholly within 12" of the bearer can attempt a charge move if they are within 15" of the enemy, and you can add 3 to their charge roll if they do so.

2   **Splintervane Broach:** *Those pierced by this shard of bone grow spiny protrusions from their flesh that absorb the flow of magic.*

Subtract 1 from casting rolls for enemy **WIZARDS** while they are within 12" of the bearer.

3   **Keening Bone:** *After this gnarled club has been hurled at an enemy, it will return to the hand of the last fiend to have tasted its juicy marrow.*

Pick one of the bearer's melee weapons. Increase the Range characteristic of this weapon to 3".

4   **The Grim Garland:** *Formed from the skulls of kings and emperors, this morbid wreath evokes fear in even the bravest champion.*

Subtract 2 from the Bravery characteristic of enemy units while they are within 6" of the bearer.

5   **Blood River Chalice:** *When the blood contained in this vessel is quaffed, the grisly fluid re-knits even the most grievous wound.*

Once per battle, at the start of your hero phase, heal D6 wounds that have been allocated to the bearer.

6   **Heart of the Gargant Feast:** *This quivering slab of flesh still beats with the strength of the gargant from which it was torn, and with each bite it bestows colossal might.*

Once per battle, at the start of the combat phase, the bearer can use this artefact. If they do so, you can re-roll failed wound rolls for the bearer in that phase.

ALLEGIANCE ABILITIES
IRONJAWZ

This section describes the allegiance abilities available to an Ironjawz army, including battle traits for the army, command traits for its general and the artefacts of power available to its heroes.

BATTLE TRAITS

Mighty Destroyers: *The Ironjawz allow nothing to stop them from getting to grips with their enemies.*

Roll a dice in your hero phase for your general and each friendly **IRONJAWZ HERO**. Add 2 to the roll for your general if they are a **MEGABOSS**. On a 6+ pick a friendly **IRONJAWZ** unit wholly within 12" of the model being rolled for. That unit can immediately make a normal move if it is more than 12" from the enemy, can immediately pile in if it is within 3" of the enemy (but not attack), and can attempt a charge in any other circumstances.

Smashing and Bashing: *When an Ironjawz mob smashes up the enemy, it inspires other mobs to emulate the feat, leading to an orgy of smashing and bashing!*

In the combat phase, after a friendly **IRONJAWZ** unit has made all of its attacks, if the attacks made by that unit resulted in any enemy units being destroyed, one friendly **IRONJAWZ** unit that has not yet fought in that combat phase can fight, instead of doing so later in the phase.

Eager for Battle: *Ironjawz are always looking for a good fight, and will not hesitate to get stuck in when they get the chance.*

Add 1 to charge rolls for friendly **IRONJAWZ** units.

COMMAND TRAITS

D6 Command Trait

1 Hulking Muscle-bound Brute: *Even by the standards of the orruks, this greenskin is enormous, and he is ever eager to throw his immense weight around in battle.*

You can re-roll wound rolls of 1 for attacks made with this general's melee weapons.

2 Live to Fight: *This orruk revels in the thick of battle, and the only times they are not in combat is when they are charging headlong into a fresh set of enemies.*

You can re-roll failed hit rolls for attacks made by this general if they charged in the same turn.

3 Brutish Cunning: *Through countless savage battles this general has learnt a few tricks to get his boyz stuck into the enemy as quickly as possible.*

Roll a dice at the start of your opponent's charge phase. On a 5+ one friendly **IRONJAWZ** unit wholly within 12" of this general can attempt to charge. This charge takes place before any enemy charges.

4 Bestial Charisma: *With a deafening bellow, this greenskin lets every orruk around know that no one leaves the fight until it's over.*

If this general is chosen as the model from which the Inspiring Presence command ability is measured, you can pick D3 units rather than 1 to be affected by the command ability.

5 Prophet of the Waaagh!: *Waves of greenskins flock to the call of this bellicose orruk, knowing that they will be led to a mighty fight.*

If this general has the Waaagh! or Mighty Waaagh! command ability, you can re-roll the dice to see if the relevant units can make an extra attack. If this general does not have one of these abilities, they can use the Waaagh! command ability from the Orruk Megaboss warscroll.

6 Ironclad: *Incoming blows bounce harmlessly off this general's impressively robust armour.*

Worsen the Rend characteristic of enemy weapons by 1, to a minimum of '-', if they target this general.

ARTEFACTS OF POWER

D6	Artefact

1 Armour of Gork: *This bashed-together armour is thick and heavy, and when it became blessed by Gork it gained its own fierce fighting spirit.*

If the save roll made for the bearer against an attack made with a melee weapon is 6+, the attacking unit suffers 1 mortal wound after all of its attacks are complete.

2 Destroyer: *This brutal weapon is surrounded by anarchic magic. It can topple a gargant or blast apart a castle wall, though once discharged its powers can only be recharged under a blood-red moon.*

Pick one of the bearer's melee weapons. Increase the weapon's Damage characteristic by 1.

3 Daubing of Mork: *Smeared onto the face or armour by a Weirdnob Shaman, the Daubing of Mork is a mark of great favour bestowed upon a particularly resilient orruk.*

Roll a dice each time a wound or mortal wound is allocated the bearer. On a 6+ the wound is negated.

4 The Golden Toof: *Amongst the Ironjawz, the Golden Toof is a symbol of great strength and ferocity, for to acquire this prized fang an orruk must first smash it out of the mouth of its previous owner.*

Friendly **Ironjawz** units that are wholly within 12" of the bearer do not have to take battleshock tests.

5 Metalrippa's Klaw: *Battered together by the Megaboss Snarlgak Metalrippa, the bladed tips of this massive iron gauntlet can tear through even the thickest armour.*

Pick one of the bearer's melee weapons. Improve the Rend characteristic of that weapon by 1.

6 The Boss Skewer: *Revered by the Ironjawz and feared by their enemies, this gigantic spike has held aloft the heads of conquered kings over many long centuries.*

Add 1 to the Bravery characteristic of friendly **Ironjawz** units while they are wholly within 18" of the bearer, and subtract 1 from the Bravery characteristic of enemy units while they are wholly within 18" of the bearer.

WARSCROLL BATTALION
IRONSUNZ

One of the largest warclans to fight in Gordrakk's Waaagh!, the Ironsunz can be seen in almost every realm, wearing flashy yellow armour and throwing their weight around to make sure that everyone knows they are the best. Megaboss Dakkbad Grotkicker has risen to rule the Ironsunz over a trail of bashed-in skulls and broken bones. Everyone knows that Dakkbad is cunning, and some orruks even reckon he might have an eye on Gordrakk's position. If the Fist of Gork is concerned about this, he hasn't let on, and if Dakkbad ever decides to have a go at usurping the Great Waaagh!, he had better make it count.

ORGANISATION

An Ironsunz battalion consists of the following:

- 1 Megaboss on Maw-krusha (Dakkbad Grotkicker)

- 1 Ironfist battalion (must contain 5 units)

An Ironsunz battalion may also contain:

- 0-4 warscroll battalions chosen in any combination from the following list:

  - Brutefist

  - Gorefist

  - Ardfist

  - Ironfist

- Any number of additional **Ironjawz** units

If an Ironsunz battalion contains the maximum number of battalions, it gains the Big Waaagh! ability from the Brawl warscroll battalion in *Battletome: Ironjawz*.

ABILITIES

Dakkbad's Cunning: *Dakkbad knows that the less his boyz get hit, the more hitting they can do. He has thus taken to launching surprise attacks at opposing armies, springing assaults with blinding speed before his foes can form into defensive positions.*

Roll a dice after set-up is complete, but before the battle begins. On a 3+ subtract 1 from hit rolls for enemy units in the first battle round.

Dakkbad's Bashing!: *Scant time passes in which Dakkbad has not felled some enemy champion, and he has a keen memory for each and every one of these fights.*

For the purposes of his Strength from Victories ability Dakkbad Grotkicker counts as already having slain an enemy **Hero** when the battle starts, with the weapon of your choice from those listed on his warscroll.